All About Riding

All About Riding

by

Clare Albinson

Contents

Why Did I Write This Book?

"... horses should be trained in such a way that they not only love their riders, but look forward to the time they are with them."   Xenophon, 400 B.C.

"We must strive for a greater understanding of the nature of our horse, his method of communication and the mechanics of his body. Most importantly we need to recognise the effect we can have on all of these. With this knowledge we can more happily co-exist and more successfully work together."   Author

We have all had the lessons, read the books and gone to the lectures. We try so hard to understand what they mean and we try to do as they say but still we don't produce horses like the top trainers. Why? What is the magic ingredient? Surely not lack of dedication, because riders are usually a very committed group of people. We tend to be well informed and so many of us watch videos and read books on the subject and have many lessons; yet success still eludes us. Why should this be? I came to the conclusion that, despite having the information at our disposal, there isn't a total understanding of that information. Perhaps fuller, better, easier to understand explanations would help us struggling equestrians learn faster.

My starting point on this book came several years ago when I volunteered to give talks on dressage to the members of our local Pony Club. I wanted to create light hearted and illuminating descriptions for the talks. Explanations occurred to me which, I felt, made what was being described surprisingly clear. At the end of the process I was amazed to find that I too had come to a better understanding of that which I was describing. At this time I was concentrating on information that explores a better understanding of the balance of the rider and the balance of the horse, how they can both be improved through training and also how the rider's balance can affect that of the horse. Understanding these concepts is fundamental to the training of the horse.

I came to realise, though, that we also need to know more about the mentality of our horses. We need to know how they relate to and communicate with each other, and therefore with us. We need to develop sympathetic training techniques which benefit both ourselves and our horses. With a better understanding of the horse's mind and an improved ability to communicate, misunderstandings between us should be reduced and our relationship improved. Schooling should become a pleasant, productive time. Understanding the instinctive behaviour of horses, and the ability to use this knowledge when schooling them, can bring enormous benefits both to the speed of progress with work as well as to the level of enjoyment experienced.

Reading this book should, hopefully, lead you to a deeper understanding of the basic balance of both you and your horse. Because you understand more about this, you will be able to direct your energy to where it is needed. The book should also lead you better to understand the mind and behaviour of your horse. If you know more about his personality, you should discover a kinder, more intelligent approach to horse training and handling, and gain a new insight into how to get the best out of your relationship.

1

Establishing Your Goals

Know where you are going

Before you bought your horse you probably had some idea
of what you wanted to achieve with him. Perhaps it was
only to ride out on the lanes and across the fields or
perhaps you wanted to hunt, event, show, show jump, do
cross country competitions or compete in dressage competitions. Some riders are content with the local shows whilst
others want to fly as high and be as successful as they can.
Sometimes these aims change either upwards with success
or downwards with increasing age and incapacity (the
voice of experience here). However humble or grand, we
need these aims and we need to know how to achieve them.

Long term goal

Do you know what you want to achieve with your horse?
Do you want to compete at local shows or the Horse of the
Year Show? Do you want your horse to do flying changes
and piaffe or would a sane, obedient horse to hack out on
be good enough for you?

If you do have a goal, have you thought how long it will
take you to get there (though this may have to be reas-
sessed constantly)? Perhaps your aim is only to become a
better rider if your horse is already where you want him to
be.

Short term goal

As well as knowing what you want to do ultimately, you
should also have an aim for the next 3 to 6 months – it is

easier to assess your progress better in shorter bursts. Some kind of a diary or journal will help you keep a better record. If you have access to a video camera and someone to film you, a video diary is even more interesting. It is good to look back and see how much you have achieved.

Even shorter term goal
The most important goal you have is the daily one – the one that you are planning in your mind as you are preparing to ride. You should have worked out exactly what you intend to achieve and more importantly how you intend to achieve it using whichever exercise, or exercises, you feel suits your horse's needs best.

You should understand what your aim is when you school a horse and why you are doing what you are doing. Schooling in a certain way, perhaps because you have seen others school in that way and their horses go well, or because you have been told that a certain exercise is good for a horse, is not necessarily the best way of schooling *your* horse. You should know why you are doing each particular exercise and what it should achieve. You must know what your horse is ready for and how he will be improved by the exercises you decide to use. They will be pointless if they do not improve him and they could damage him if he is not physically ready. Every exercise has a particular effect on the anatomical development of the horse and you must know these exercises and their effect if you are to use them correctly. You should also know how a horse should look and feel if he is working correctly, and therefore recognise if he is not working correctly and why. You should then be able to devise a method of schooling that is directly aimed at putting this right.

Sometimes you may even adopt unconventional methods to achieve your ends. You should know how your horse ticks, mentally and physically. Because you know how particular exercises will affect the way your horse performs, you should be able to work out a system of training that suits your horse as an individual and be able to devise methods of solving your problems when they appear.

Evaluate your horse

Before you start work, properly evaluate your horse, physically and mentally. You must know his weaknesses – look at his body. Does he throw a lot of his weight on his forehand? Has he a lot of muscle under his neck and none on top? Is he bossy or is he timid? Is he highly strung or calm? When you are riding him on a circle does he easily bend his body in the direction you are going? Does he bend better to one side than the other – if so, which side? Is he stiff and/or sluggish? Look also at your riding and observe your strengths and weaknesses – are you balanced, do you sit deeply enough and are you holding the reins correctly? There is so much to know about both of you.

When you decide what direction your training should take, bear in mind your horse's general conformation and for the most part work in an opposite way to that conformation. For example, if your horse is physically very strong and muscled the chances are he will not be particularly supple. You should concentrate, therefore, on exercises that will increase his flexibility and overall suppleness. If he is naturally supple he will probably not be strong and therefore you should concentrate on increasing his physical strength. If he turns easily to the right you will spend more time working him on the left rein to make him as supple on the left as on the right.

It would take many, many pages to cover all the possible deficiencies you may see and feel in your horse or may exist in yourself. The point is that you must be constantly examining both of you to know what they may be. You can ask others, particularly your trainer, what they feel they are. Knowing his weaknesses, and your weaknesses, means you are able to develop a programme of work that will help you and your horse improve.

Assessing the results

After each and every training session, before you do anything else, you should ask yourself how well you have achieved your goal and if the work you have chosen to do was correct. If perhaps another route may be more beneficial, try that next time. Or be prepared to stick with the original scheme if you think all that is needed is more time. Rome wasn't built in a day and you won't build your horse's physique and train him to his potential in a day, a week, a month or even a year. This is no job for the faint hearted or weak of character.

When assessing the results of your work be prepared, if necessary, to admit error and adjust your methods if what you are doing is not working out the way it should.

It is very difficult to evaluate your horse properly or assess his progress while you are riding. This is particularly true of flat work but it is also very helpful to have someone on the ground to watch and/or help you when you are jumping. Someone on the ground is able to see so much more than you will be able to feel as a rider. Obviously the more knowledgeable this person, the more help he can be to you. This is why most riders have someone to help them on a regular basis. The better the helper or trainer, and the more often he helps or trains, the faster the rider will progress. Obviously this can be expensive but it should be worth the cost if you wish to succeed. An alternative, or supplement, to regular lessons is the use of a video camera. Filming your progress at intervals is a much more accurate way to assess your progress than gauging it from your riding.

Early correct training

Your first job is to lay down the very firm foundations of correct work. It is worth taking time over each step to make sure it is correct and established. The net result will be faster progress. When you are teaching your horse to do something new, don't be satisfied with anything less than correct work. Even though you want to get on to the next topic quickly, be patient, make yourself wait until your lesson is established and true. This doesn't mean slog at that particular lesson for the whole of the training period. It should be part of other work, mostly work that he performs happily. Every day you will work for some time on the new exercise hoping for an improvement on each occasion.

A horse's memory is so good that once the lesson is taught it will not be forgotten, so it is worth getting it right.

It is also worth teaching the lesson carefully and kindly because the impact of a lesson that caused tension, discomfort or pain will always be recalled and the memory of those feelings will return when the movement is required again. Sometimes you may feel that you are boring him, going over and over the same thing until it is right. Could it be you that may be getting a little bored? Horses often cope with boredom quite well.

Remember that the less you rush, the quicker you will proceed. A short lesson that achieves anything, even if it is only a little, is worth a lot. If every lesson achieves a little then, day by day, when small achievement is added to small achievement, your total achievement will be great. Some days you need to be happy with merely consolidating yesterday's achievement but as long as you are going forwards and not backwards you should be pleased. But there will be many days when the work does seem to be going backwards. Do not allow this to make you despondent. It happens to most trainers and most horses. View your setbacks objectively and reason what the cause is. It will be easier to stay calm and to resist the temptation to get angry with yourself or your horse if you know why it has happened. If you can understand the cause of the setback you can feel that you have learnt from the experience and not lost by it.

The development of the horse's training can be divided into five stages.

1. Teaching your horse fundamental discipline.
2. Teaching him to understand basic aids.
(The teaching of the rest of the aids is progressive throughout the training of the horse.)
3. Establishing work on the bit.
4. Keeping your horse in the correct outline while developing the energetic activation of the hind legs and by encouraging the horse to step further under his own weight by the use of exercises.
5. Developing this even further by harnessing the forward energy with the collecting ability of the reins, so that the hind legs now begin to take a slightly greater proportion of the weight of the horse by coming under the horse

and lowering the quarters. The horse now takes on a shorter, more compressed outline.

Working in and working down

So many people come straight out of the stable or horse box and set off immediately at a spanking trot. I think this must be a little like leaping out of bed in a morning and immediately jogging round the block. When you first get out of bed your body is relatively stiff – you know instinctively that to throw yourself into vigorous exercise at this time would be uncomfortable and risk injury. Instead you would stretch and then move around gently. When the horse comes out of the stable, trailer or horse box his body will also be a little stiff. He deserves time to warm up gently without any effort being involved. This is called working in. Because of the density of tissue, a more muscular horse will often require more time than a lithe, slim horse.

Working in satisfies two needs. Firstly it should warm the horse's body tissue so that it becomes more flexible and therefore more able to stretch and remain undamaged during exercise. Secondly the working in starts the process of stretching the horse's body so that it is able to use itself better during work.

If a horse warms up gently, both his body and his brain will benefit. He will be thinking to himself – "this is easy". Gradually increase the energy of the work but keep it relaxed and easy. If the horse thinks the work is easy he will relax. A relaxed body and brain will perform so much better than a tense or stiff horse.

Working down

After you have worked, work down. This is particularly necessary if you have worked muscles hard as it disperses the lactic acid that can be produced by hard work. Doing this will reduce the likelihood of cramps and muscle stiffness. Working down is merely finishing the work off with easy, relaxed exercise, stretching muscles gently and keeping the blood pumping around the body a little faster than it would when standing still. It is the reverse of working in.

Consistency of training

When horses are given options it tends to confuse them. They prefer clear directions and consistency in their directions so that they know exactly what is wanted from their rider. If on some occasions the horse is allowed to disobey the rider, the horse will feel that he has a choice as to whether he obeys commands or not.

A horse cannot be allowed to do what he wants when you are riding him. Perhaps he has developed a habit of stopping when you haven't asked him or breaking out of canter or into canter without your giving the aid. If you do not correct him immediately he will think he is being given the choice of what he wants to do. This ability to choose is not good for the horse. A horse ridden like this will become gradually more and more disobedient and will always choose the easy way out if he thinks there is a choice. It creates a feeling of uncertainty and hesitation. This type of riding almost always belongs in the world of the amateur who often feels, mistakenly, that he or she is being kind to the horse. The opposite is in fact true. The horse will feel much happier and more secure when his rider knows exactly what he wants and insists on it. He will be much less stressed and therefore more relaxed when ridden positively.

How long should each training session last?

What criteria should you use when deciding how long to work your horse? Should it be the goal you set yourself to achieve or should it be the fitness of the horse?

The first consideration will be the goal you set yourself but this will be dominated by the fitness of the horse. How much work you do at a time is a mixture of preplanning and assessing things as you go. If the horse learns the lesson more quickly than you had expected, finish the lesson there. He has done well and finishing early is his reward. If it turns out that your horse is not learning as quickly as you expected, or if you feel he is tiring, finish on the best note you can and then resume your work in the next session.

One of the most difficult things to assess when working

15

a horse is what the horse is actually capable of doing – you don't wish to overstrain him but you do want to stretch him. No one can tell you this; it is something you must feel for yourself. A fair rule of thumb as regards tiredness is wait until your horse says he is tired and then do some more – not a massive amount but just enough to know that you have pushed the boundaries of his fitness. In the same way, if he manages an exercise easily, try another exercise that will stretch him a little more. Constantly look for a stretching of his abilities and fitness without straining him or over facing him.

How often should you train?
You need to decide how much time you will spend on your horse's training and work out a regular routine.

Some people work their horses six or seven days a week but it is debatable whether there is any great advantage in this relatively demanding schedule. How much and how often you train depends on the age of your horse and on what you are trying to teach him. Recently backed horses do need to be worked frequently because they have to get used to the idea of being ridden. Being worked for a short time every day helps them quickly to overcome the strange feeling of having someone on their back. All the lessons you teach them at this stage should be physically and mentally very easy – they have enough on their plate learning to carry a human.

If the work is physically undemanding, daily lessons will not cause any strain. If, however, there were to be the slightest chance that the work may involve strain, which may result in stiffness or tiredness, it would not be wise to work hard the following day. If work has been hard you run the risk of putting further strain on an already strained part of the body which may well result in injury. In this situation exercise should be confined to relaxing, easy work. When we don't know if they will be stiff or not we have to err on the side of caution.

You must judge for yourself what regime you will follow – a lot will depend on your time and also on the horse himself – some horses like the routine of daily work and work more sanely because of it. Other horses will resent the boredom of daily work. Most horses are fresher for a day or two off or the occasional days spent hacking. This is where the advantage of knowing your horse comes in.

Resting between work will help to keep your horse working well. Usually these rests are for periods of 20 to 30 seconds. Some horses will benefit from occasional longer rests when they could stand or walk on a loose rein. When they start work again they are fresher and have more energy. However, not all horses benefit from rests as some will stiffen up and perform less well particularly after a long rest – you have to try it to know. Resting your horse is quite a good way to reward him if he has performed well or worked hard for you.

Finish on a good note

Whenever you are working your horse, make sure that the last thing you do with him is good and worthy of praise, which should be freely given. If you have been teaching him something he doesn't like too much or that he finds difficult, or if he has been in a poor mood and not worked well, go to something that he likes and does well. When he has performed it well, praise him and stop work. The horse will come out to his next training session with the memory of how the last one finished, and if he has a good memory will approach it with a good feeling. As a rider it will also affect your approach to the lesson bringing a happy, positive feel to it.

2

Better Riding

The balanced rider

A good rider must be balanced. A balanced rider will be able to stay on the back of the horse without hanging onto the reins or the saddle and won't be gripping the sides of the horse with the legs. A balanced rider will distribute his or her weight equally over the horse's back. He or she will not lean sideways, forwards or backwards so that there will be no inbalance of weight to interfere with the horse's own balance and way of going.

What is balance?

In this instance it is having an equality of weight either side of the centre of support. In the case of a human being, when you are standing your legs must be situated centrally under the weight of your body. If there is more weight on one side than the other you may fall over. In order to stop yourself falling over you may tense the muscles in your legs or feet or you move one of your legs under that unsupported weight.

The person in fig.1 is out of balance because there is too much weight to the left of the central line drawn above the supporting leg(s). In the case of figure A, if she doesn't wish to fall over, she will either tense her toes and the muscles at the front of her legs or support the unbalanced weight by stepping forwards. In the case of figure B if she wishes to remain upright she must step with her right leg to the left so that she is putting a support under the unbalanced, extra weight on the left.

18

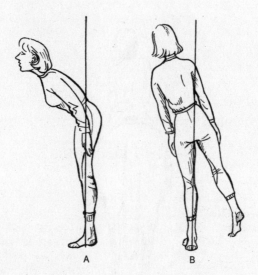

Fig. 1 Out of balance.

You need to look at the body of the rider from the side (lateral balance) and from the back (lineal balance) to see if he or she is in balance.

Lateral balance
Viewed from the back it should be possible to draw a vertical line upward from a point equidistant from each of the horse's back legs. This line should pass up along the tail and spine of the horse then up the spine of the rider and eventually dissect the rider's head. The rider should have as much weight on one side of that line as on the other.

The rider in fig. 2 has too much weight over her right hip joint and is therefore putting more weight on the right hand side of the horse than on the left.

The rider in fig. 3 is well balanced on the horse.

Lineal balance
There should be an equal amount of weight placed in front of and behind an imaginary line going up vertically from the back of the heel. If a rider is balanced this line should

Fig. 2 Too much weight over right hip.

go vertically upwards from the heel and pass through the hip, elbow, shoulder and ear of the rider. If there is too much weight in front of the centre line, as would be the case with a rider sitting on the fork, or with a rider who looks down, more weight than should be will be placed over the horse's forehand. If there is too much weight behind that line, as is the case with a rider possessing an armchair seat, the rider is unable to sit deeply in the saddle and the legs tend to hang rather ineffectively down the sides of the horse.

You should put most of your weight directly onto your seat bones. To achieve this, place your hands underneath your seat bones and allow your weight to drop onto them. You should feel this weight pressing down on your hands. Take your hands away and still feel the weight of your body pushing onto the saddle. Whether you are sitting or

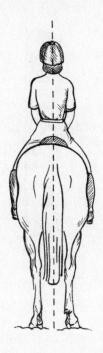

Fig. 3 Well balanced.

riding you should always have your weight on these seat bones if you are to be in balance. When you are riding, your weight should be placed firmly on these seat bones and your legs should hang down long by the horse's sides. Some of your weight should go down your leg to the ball of your foot which should be placed firmly into and onto the stirrups. Fig. 4A shows this.

A fork seat. Fig. 4B. A rider who sits on his or her fork is not in a secure position. Here the rider pushes the hips forwards and virtually sits over the fork of the legs. With too much weight forward of the centre line, the rider will be easily pulled out of the saddle by a horse that takes a hold or pulls on the reins. This rider's seat has very little contact with the saddle. Because of this and because of

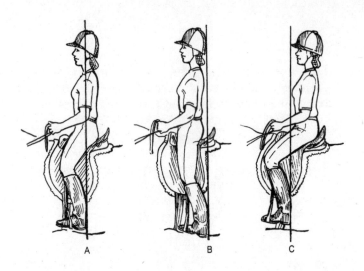

Fig. 4
A Correct seat.
B Fork seat.
C Armchair seat.

the angle of the body it will be impossible to relax into the rhythm of the horse.

The armchair seat. Fig. 4C. This is quite the opposite of the fork seat because the rider puts too much weight on his or her bottom rather than on the seat bones. The legs go forwards of the body, as if sitting in an armchair, and do not hang well down the horse's sides. Some of the rider's weight should pass down the legs but with this seat it all stops at the saddle. The rider has to rely on the upper part of the body alone to achieve balance. The rider's weight is well behind the vertical and hence will be easily tipped backwards. The rider will not feel secure and will often seek the reins as a source of support.

It is very much worthwhile asking someone to look at you from the side and the back while you ride and check that you are sitting in a balanced position. It is virtually impossible to tell if you are out of balance without such help because you get so used to a position, even if it is wrong, and your body may have made unnoticed compensations ages ago.

Your body is programmed to stop you from falling over or falling off and often will make adjustments without you realising that you have done anything. Sometimes, if you are out of balance, instead of putting the balance right you will tense another part of your body to keep yourself from falling off – often you will not have realised that you have done this, so instinctive is the reaction. This means it is possible to walk and ride with more weight on one side of your body than the other and be unaware of it. To remain upright when you are out of balance your body will have had to tense muscles. This tension will possibly affect your whole body. Remember how your toes and calves tensed when you leaned forwards slightly. As a non-riding human this imbalance can place strain on your body causing eventual damage – particularly to the spine. The unbalanced rider can put a disproportionate amount of weight on one side of the horse causing the horse to be out of balance. For example, if when you were riding you were out of balance and leaning to one side, you would be putting more weight on that side of the horse, which would make him unbalanced on that side. This lack of balance will make him uncomfortable, tense and desirous of balancing himself by taking a step to the right.

There are several detrimental consequences of being an unbalanced rider:

Gripping. Because you are not evenly balanced you will feel as if you are going to fall off the horse and your legs will grip to hold you on the horse. This gripping will stop you from having a deep seat – gripping legs push you to the top of the saddle. You have the most effective seat if your legs are open and relaxed which allows you to sit deeply in the saddle having the maximum contact with the horse's body.

If you are gripping, it means there is tension in some part of your body. Tension stops you from being relaxed. It is essential for a rider to be relaxed. This is partly because

23

tension will communicate itself to the horse and also because a relaxed rider will be able to sit deeply in the saddle and feel the movement of the horse, whereas a tense rider will not. If you are relaxed you will become part of the movement of the horse and sense better what is happening beneath you. If you have tension in your body this will not be possible.

Gripping confuses the clarity of the leg aids. The legs should only gently touch the sides of the horse. When the leg aids are applied, the legs should merely increase their contact or pressure to give a message to the horse. If, however, the legs are already applying pressure to the sides of the horse, because you are gripping, then there is no margin for increasing this pressure to tell the horse what you want.

Ineffective riding. A lopsided rider is obviously less secure than he/she should be and therefore could not ride the horse effectively. He/she will be aware that he/she is not totally secure and some attention will be given to staying on the horse even though unaware of it. This will still be true even if the rider is leaning only by a small degree. There will be more concern about staying on the horse than about riding him well and those gripping legs will want to stay in the same position on the horse's sides and not be able to move around, as they need to if giving precise aids.

Weight. The horse will know if there is more weight on one side of his body than on the other – he will feel that you are about to fall off and his instinctive reaction will be to take a step in the direction of the potential fall to catch your weight.

Try imagining, or actually, carrying a small child on your shoulders (fig. 5). When that child leans to one side your immediate reaction is to take a step in the direction in which the child is leaning, to step under the weight of the child. The horse will want to do the same thing. We can use this displacement of weight as an aid if we want the horse to move sideways but if we want to go in a straight line it is most important to keep our balance absolutely central.

Fig. 5 Try carrying a small child on your shoulders.

Weight of the head

Many riders look down when they are riding, largely to check on what they and the horse are doing. Because we are so used to looking down we think nothing of it and don't realise that it affects our and the horse's way of going. In fact, the head weighs over 14lbs and, if we are looking down, it seriously affects both our balance and the horse's balance. In the case of the horse we are placing all this extra weight over his forehand and therefore putting more weight where we wish there to be less weight.

The Alexander Technique can be of enormous help in improving our balance including as a rider. It is a technique that is becoming much more popular and hence more available. For details of teachers in your area contact The Society of Teachers of the Alexander Technique (for address see Appendix page 283).

A DEEP SEAT

Why do you need a deep seat?

Initially so that you can stay on better – if your legs are hanging long either side of the horse and you are not perched on the top like a pea on a drum you will feel more secure and therefore more relaxed on the horse.

Because you feel more secure you are not gripping with your legs to stay on and as we have seen there are many disadvantages to gripping.

Because you feel more secure you will relax into the movement of the horse. You will feel his movement and interpret how he is going. You will be able to learn to go with his movement which is easier for the horse. Horse and rider will move as one.

What is a deep seat?
It is a seat where the hip-bones of the rider are opened slightly so that the legs are able to have as much contact as possible with the saddle. From the hips down, the whole of the length of the legs should wrap themselves gently around the sides of the horse.

How to obtain a deep seat
When you first sit in the saddle put your hand under the pommel and pull yourself deeper into the saddle. Wriggle your body downwards allowing your hips to open slightly and push your pelvis a little forward so that you feel you are as far down in the saddle as you could be. At the same time as you are trying to get your lower body deep into the saddle your upper body needs to grow and be as tall as you can make it. Imagine there is a string attached to the top of your head pulling you higher and stretching the middle of your body. While someone is holding your horse put your hands underneath your seat bones. Push hard down on your hands so that they can feel the shape of the bones pressing on them. Take your hands away and try and keep the feeling of the bones pressing down on the saddle. For the moment do not take up the stirrups. Allow your legs to hang down the sides of the horse, turn your toes downward and try and reach the ground with them. Push down on both toes to get them as near to the ground as you can. Try and make your legs as long as possible. Do not grip with your legs just let them hang long around the horse's sides. In a safe place ride your horse first in walk then in trot. Use

the movement of the horse in walk to help you get even deeper into the saddle. When you trot try not to let the strength of the horse's stride throw you up out of the saddle. Try to feel the rhythm of the horse and move with it and into it, flexing your back with the movement of the horse. It will be even more beneficial if you could have an assistant to lunge your horse while you are riding without stirrups. You will be able to relax better – you will be safer and you will be able to give more concentration to what you are doing. When you retake your stirrups, their height will lift your toes upwards – you should never make a conscious effort to lift your toes. Always work to have your legs as long as possible and let the stirrups take care of the toes.

Lungeing is a method of schooling a horse from the ground. The, normally riderless, horse is attached to one end of a 10 metre (32 yard) rein while the trainer holds the other end of the rein and works the horse around him in a circle. It is a very useful way of schooling horses particularly before they are ridden. The technique is difficult to describe in a book and is best done by, or learnt from, a trainer who is experienced in lungeing.

Below are a series of exercises that will help you achieve a deeper seat. As with the one above they will achieve more if they are ridden at walk and trot. Even when you feel you have achieved a deep seat these exercises are very beneficial and worth repeating every so often to keep your seat as deep as possible.

Exercise A (See overleaf.)
Still riding without your stirrups imagine there is a heavy weight attached to your legs pulling them downwards. You should feel your thighs stretching and moulding themselves around the top of the saddle and your legs getting longer and longer.

Exercise B (See overleaf.)
While your legs are out of the stirrups put one hand on your head and push downwards. At the same time push up against the weight of the hand to sit as tall as you can. Now

Fig. 6 Exercise A.

Fig. 7 Exercise B.

imagine the weight of your hand travelling down your head into your body and into your legs. It should end up feeling like heavy weights on the end of your toes pulling them down towards the ground and making your legs as long as they possibly could be.

Exercise C

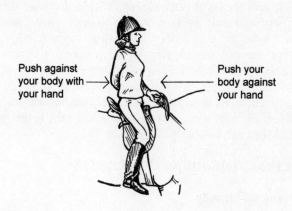

Push against your body with your hand →

← Push your body against your hand

Fig. 8 Exercise C.

Place one hand in the small of your back and push against your back. At the same time push against your hand with your body.

Leg Contact
When you have achieved a good, deep seat your legs should merely hang down the horse's sides with a slight contact – they should not grip in any way. It may feel more secure to grip the horse's sides with your legs, but when you grip you cannot sit deeply into the saddle. Imagine your legs were a finger and thumb and imagine the horse was an egg with butter on the outside. If you tried to grip the egg around the middle, your fingers would slide right up to the top. Like your fingers on the egg, your squeezing legs will push the horse away from you and leave you perched on the top of the horse rather than sitting deeply in the saddle.

The rider's legs should not grip the horse but neither

should they hang away from the sides of the horse. They should wrap themselves gently around the curve of the horse's body so that there is a light contact with his sides at all times. Because there is always some slight contact, the horse is aware of the potentially guiding presence of the legs. It also means it is easier for the rider to make the leg aids very subtle. If the legs hung a distance away from the horse's sides the action of bringing them to the horse's side to give the aid would tend to be rougher, sharper and probably more sudden. This will make the reaction of the horse similarly rough and sharp. Because the legs are already close to the horse, the aids can be smooth and subtle. If the aids are given smoothly and subtly, the horse should respond smoothly and subtly.

HOLDING THE REINS CORRECTLY

Keeping still hands

When you first start to ride you feel very insecure, you feel you are bobbing around all over the place and likely to fall off at any moment. Most learners hang on to the reins as if they will give some stability and keep them on the horse. Because their bodies are bouncing uncontrollably, their hands will bounce with them, risking jabbing the horse in the mouth with the bit. Fortunately most of such novice riders also have long reins so that the reins held by those bouncing hands should not pull at and jar the mouths of the horse they are riding.

As we get better at riding and our seat becomes more balanced, we start to feel more secure in the saddle and less reliant on the reins for support. But, even though we don't feel we need the support of the reins to stay on the horse, some of us have difficulty in separating the movement of our bodies from the movement of our hands. If our bodies bounce up and down with the horse's movement, our hands also go up and down. If our hands go up and down they may be catching the horse in the mouth (unless we have very long reins) and they certainly wouldn't be able to maintain a constant contact with the reins. Needless to say if we were riding like this we would be at our worst during the trot because the action of the horse in trot is the most unseating. A good rider needs to be able to separate the movement of the body from the movement of the hands. The hands and the body need to operate and move independently of each other.

It is difficult to know how independent one's own hands are because when you look at them they tend to behave themselves and stay still. But you don't know what they are doing when you aren't looking! Here is how you can test your ability to separate the movements of your body and your hands. Put a full glass of water in each hand and then jump up and down quite vigorously (but not when you are riding). If you can keep all the water in the glass this is good. Even though the rest of you has been moving all over the place your hands have stayed still. When you landed on the ground you absorbed the motion of the jump with your ankles, knees, hips, elbows and wrists and didn't allow the motion to pass into your hands – they remained still. Your hands need to be as still as this when you are riding. If you are unable to keep them still, your contact with the horse's mouth is not as smooth and independent as it should be, and you may be catching your horse in the mouth.

To improve your ability to separate the movement of your body and hands, ask a friend to lunge your horse while you are riding. Drop the reins but position your hands in front of you as if you were still holding them – lower your eyes to look at them from time to time to check that you are not moving them. Your friend will probably be happy to tell you what they are doing. Just as when you held the glass full of water you need to absorb the movement of the horse into your own body without letting it pass into your hands. The movement needs to be absorbed by your back, shoulders and elbows but most particularly by your back. If you are doing it properly you will notice the lower part of your back and your stomach moving backwards and forwards as you absorb the movement. If you want to know how good you are at this, and you are sure your horse won't get upset, put two eggs (chalk eggs preferably) on two spoons. See if you can keep them both in place while holding them out in front of you (as if you were doing the egg and spoon race).

How tight should the reins be?

The first guide one is given to help judge the tension of the reins is that they should be as taut as a piece of elastic stretched. You shouldn't pull hard on the reins but neither should the contact you have with the horse's mouth be too gentle and soft. Certainly they should be held strongly enough to make sure that neither rein loops at any time. Having said this it is still difficult to describe exactly how tight the reins should be held. This is partly because there is no hard and fast rule. Sometimes you will need to increase the strength of contact if perhaps the horse is fighting your control but when the horse relaxes onto the bit you will need to lessen it. However, one needs a starting point – a guide to an average strength of contact. Having achieved this the rider can then alter it as his proficiency develops. As time goes on, the rider will develop a feel of the reins, and of the horse's mouth beyond them. He or she will become more intuitive and more able to judge the strength of contact that is needed.

For the time being I will suggest a *very general* guide to how tight the reins should be. Wrap a sponge around a pillar tap, or other fixed narrow upright of around an inch in diameter. Put a rein or lead rope around the outside of the sponge and hold either end as if they were reins. The sponge should be about 8 inches by 4 inches by 2 inches thick and not of a dense constituency. A large car sponge is the most ideal. Bring the reins towards you until the insides of the sponge have touched each other. This, very generally speaking, is the strength of contact required when holding the reins. See fig. 9.

There is another way of deciding how tightly held the reins should be. I'm sure you know that a horse should work on the bit (see Chapter 3, page 66). When the horse is working on the bit his head is roughly speaking vertical to the ground. The way you hold your reins will often determine whether or not the horse is working on the bit. If they are too soft he will lift his head in the air. While he is

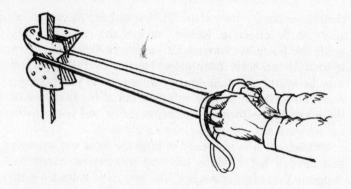

Fig. 9 The strength of contact required.

standing still (when he will find it easy) ask your horse to lower his head so that he is on the bit. While his head is there make sure that your reins go straight from his mouth to your hands without a loop. The position that your hands are in now should be correct. The length of rein should also be correct. Memorise it and keep to it. Hold them firmly in this position and don't let him move them. He must understand that he has to be the one to give in and put his head where you want it. He may think otherwise and want to pull your arms out of your sockets. If so, hold firm – he must be the one to give in. It is possible that you have a very strong contact at this stage if the horse is fighting. Stick it out for some time – eventually it should soften as the horse gives in. If he doesn't give in and ends up leaning on your hands constantly, abandon this method – you will have to find another way of getting him onto the bit. He is using your hands to support him – your arms will ache from the effort and he will not be learning to support himself.

If you are lucky your horse may be very happy to work on the bit. When his head is in the correct position you can reward him by lightening your strength of contact.

Strength of contact is not an easy subject to understand or explain. Because we don't want to damage the horse's mouth we have a natural inclination to hold the reins too softly to be effective. Remember that the reins not only guide the horse but harness his energy as well. They have to restrain the horse from going too fast even though you may be asking for more energy from him. If you hold the reins too softly the energy will flow out of the front end of the horse in the form of increased speed and not convert the forward motion into an elevating energy.

Conversely it is also easy to hold the reins too strongly and have a horse which ends up using your hands for support. You must never feel like you have a dead weight in your hands. The contact, though positive and constant, should be elastic and sympathetic. Just as you feed your horse with information through the reins he can also feed you with information about how he feels – it is a two-way system. If the reins are held too strongly they become heavy and dead and you will not feel any communication from him except to tell you that he is using the reins for support. A contact with the reins that is too strong will encourage a horse to lean on them and not balance himself.

Some horses tend to create heavy hands in their riders – they are usually those horses who rush everywhere and are too forward going for their stage of training to keep their balance. Their riders spend most of their time desperately trying to slow them down with the reins because they are going so fast and feel out of control. Their speed throws a lot of weight on the forehand and they feel very unbalanced. Unfortunately, if you have been using strong hands to stop them from rushing off, they begin to rely on your hands for support – your hands are the balancing agent. The only way to stop this vicious circle is to make them find their own balance by not allowing them to take support from the reins. In other words you reduce the amount of contact you have with the reins. If your horse is rushing or going so fast that you feel you need to slow them down, do this. Use your reins, your legs and your back to make the horse go at the speed you wish. When he is going more slowly, soften your contact. When he speeds up again, which he will almost certainly do, slow him down again and, when he responds, reduce your strength of contact. This will probably go on for some time before he gets the message and goes at your pace the whole of the time without leaning on the reins. This is because his conformation makes it difficult for him to support his own weight and he will only truly improve when you are able to correct his balance using the exercises later on in the book.

The wall

When a horse is unbalanced, the great amount of weight on his forehand feels like it is pushing his nose down towards the ground and he is heavy and cumbersome in front. The weight driving him forwards makes it difficult to control his speed. The way for him to balance himself would be to put his back legs further under him, but because he finds this difficult he takes the easy option and remains unbalanced. To him it feels absolutely natural and the right way to go. If you try to control the speed by holding more tightly onto the reins he will happily accept this and will lean on them because they are helping to support the weight of his forehand. Your hands are making life easier for him but they are not making life easier for you. After a while your arms will ache and the horse will never help himself to be better balanced while you are giving him this support.

To understand how the horse feels in this situation: stand about a metre away from a wall – allow yourself to tip forwards towards the wall. What do you instinctively do to stop yourself from falling over? You put your arms out and catch your weight by putting your hands on the wall.

Take a step backwards so that you are about two metres away from the wall now. Again tip forwards towards the wall – you are falling over but the wall is too far away for you to reach it. What is your instinctive reaction this time? It should be to put a foot forwards to catch your weight. Putting this foot under your falling body will stop you from hitting the ground. Fig.10 shows these.

The reins should be straight

The reins should always be in a straight line between your hands and the bit so that you always have a feel of, or a

Fig. 10
(Above) Catch your weight by putting your hands against the wall.
(Below) The wall is too far away, so you have to put your foot forward.

contact with, the horse's mouth. This means there must be some tension in the reins otherwise they would loop and there would not be an immediate communication system with the mouth of the horse. There must be a sufficient strength of contact to keep them straight and unlooped. This is illustrated in fig. 11.

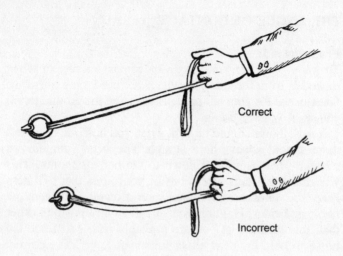

Correct

Incorrect

Fig. 11 Tension of the reins.

The reins can be compared to the steering wheel of a car. When you are driving you hold onto it continuously, not just when you are going round a bend or turning, but also when you are going in a straight line. If you don't, the car will go its own way – it is lacking direction from you. Some people hold the horse's reins but only have a proper contact with the horse's mouth when they want to turn or stop. The rest of the time they allow the reins to slacken and so do not have a contact with the horse's mouth – they have shut down communication with him – directional control has been handed to the horse.

You must always have a contact with the horse's mouth. If you move your hands by even a small degree he should be able to feel that movement and respond to it. You should be constantly in contact or communication with him even when you are asking him to carry on doing what he was already doing. While he can feel your touch on his mouth he is listening to you and waiting for further orders.

THE ANGLE OF CONTACT

From the side

To know whether your angle of contact is correct when looked at from the side you will either need a big mirror so you can see for yourself or an assistant on the ground to tell you what you are doing.

Your elbows should be bent when you hold the reins and there should always be a straight line from your elbows through your hands and down to the horse's mouth. This will make the reins extensions of your arms that will help keep the lines of communication flowing between the horse and rider. Holding your hands in any position other than this means that you are probably trying to force the horse to hold his head either higher or lower. The correct angle is shown in fig. 12, while those in fig. 13 are wrong.

Fig. 12 The correct angle of contact.

If there is no bend in the elbow and the arm is straight the hand will be held low. In this position the contact becomes fixed and inflexible. It will be lacking in ability both to send and receive messages to and from the horse. It is very easy to get into the habit of holding the reins like this when the horse is resisting being on the bit. Though it

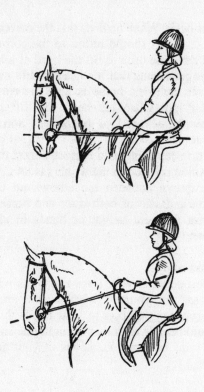

Fig. 13 Incorrect angles of contact.

does give you a little more control it is not the way to overcome the problem – the horse should be taught to accept the control of the bit with the hands in the normal position.

Holding the reins so that the hands are lifted above the straight line is usually an attempt by the rider to lift the horse's head. Sometimes it is acceptable to do this – if perhaps the horse has a tendency to lower his head too far or perhaps if he is coming behind the bit. When the reins are lifted it puts an upward pressure on the corner of the lips and asks the horse to lift his head but it should only be used as a correction. In other words if the horse's head is too low you may lift your hands until the horse obliges you by lifting his head. When he does this the correction should stop and your hands should return to the correct position. This should never be used to lift the head of a horse whose stage of training means that his head should still be low – you must wait until the horse is able to bring his hocks further under him when his head will lift naturally. It should never be allowed to become a normal way of holding the reins.

There is no such thing as a correct height of the hands. Their position in relation to the withers is totally dependent on the line drawn between the elbow and the bit. The conformation and size of both rider and horse will there-fore dictate a different height of hands in almost every case.

Viewed from above
You can look down at your arms and reins while you are riding and see for yourself whether you are doing this correctly. From your elbows to your hands through to the bit you should be able to draw a straight line so that, just as before, the reins become extensions of your arms. This is shown in fig.14.

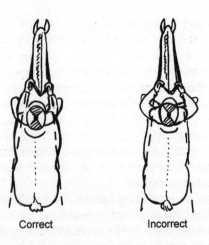

Correct   Incorrect

Fig. 14 You should be able to draw a straight line . . .

The position of the hands

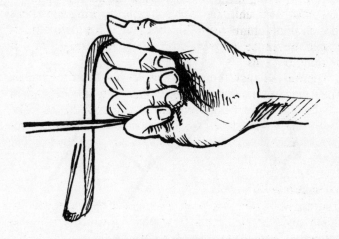

Fig. 15 The correct position of the hands.

They should be fists upwards as shown in fig. 15. If they are held like this the rider has maximum flexibility of the fingers, wrist and elbows. The reins can be shortened or extended by bending or unbending the fingers, the wrists and/or the elbows. Pretend you are holding the reins as in fig. 15. By bending the joints of the fingers, wrist and elbow see just how much effect one can have on the length of the reins.

Now turn your hands down so that your knuckles are uppermost and your fingers are facing the withers of the horse, as shown in fig.16.

Your fingers, wrists and elbows now have very little flexibility. They have become virtually rigid and you have minimal ability to alter your contact. Try to bend your fingers, wrists and elbows – you will find them so much more restricted than before.

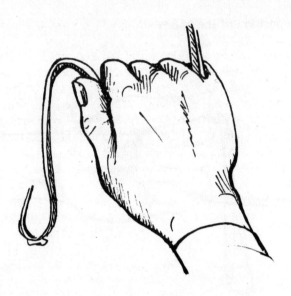

Fig. 16 Your hands should not be turned down.

The rider's back

A rider's back should be supple and mobile – it should absorb the shock of the movement of your body onto the horse's back caused by the up and down movement of the horse. When your body makes a contact with the saddle your back and neck should collapse slightly to absorb the concussion that would otherwise follow. To ride like this makes the horse more comfortable. You can imagine that a rider with a rigid, unsupple back would cause a degree of pain or discomfort as he or she bounced heavily onto the back of the horse. Obviously it is our intention to minimise this discomfort because we care about the horse and want him to work as well as possible. If he is waiting for the next crashing bounce of the rider he will be bracing his back, rather as you would brace the muscles of your stomach if you knew someone was about to punch you there. If he is bracing his back like this it cannot be as supple, relaxed and as stretched as it needs to be for him to round his back and work properly.

If the back of the rider is relaxed and moving with the rhythm of the horse, the rider almost becomes part of the horse and will be very responsive to any changes in the horse's way of going. He or she can feel the movement of the horse and if anything is wrong with that movement or rhythm. If the rider is a part of the horse's movement, the horse will be more able to detect any differences in the rider's seat such as when he or she uses the back as a driving aid or braces the back as a blocking aid. When you ride, imagine you can feel the movement of each of the horse's back legs coming underneath him, lifting him and in turn lifting you. You should be able to feel the power and lift of the right leg of the horse lifting your right hip and of the left leg lifting your left hip.

As a driving aid

As described above, when the horse is moving, the rider collapses the back slightly to absorb the movement of the horse. When the back is at its most collapsed state, instead of coming back into an upright position, the rider pushes even further down into the saddle in an exaggerated movement pushing the pelvis forwards and down. This aid can be repeated each time that the rider collapses his or her back until the horse is as forward going as is intended. Normally the rider would follow the rhythm and movement of the horse but when the back is used as a driving aid it is asking the horse to lengthen his rhythm by sustaining the length and strength of the downward motion. This encourages the horse to take longer, stronger steps with his hind legs.

A braced back

A relaxed mobile back encourages the horse to work forwards fluently. The rider is following the movement and rhythm of the horse. A braced back is the opposite, it is an immobile back, a back that does not go with the rhythm of the horse. It is a back that cuts across the rhythm of the horse's movement and makes forward movement relatively unpleasant for him. It is very easy for the horse to understand that the rider wants him to stop moving in the manner that he is, because it makes continuing uncomfortable for him. The braced back is used in the transitions down. It is only used until that split second when the horse drops out of the faster pace into the slower pace, as it is important that forward movement is continued as soon as that slower pace is achieved. If the back were to remain braced the horse would, at worst, stop all forward movement and, at best, not be forward going in the pace you had selected. Even if the downward transition was to halt, the braced back should not be maintained, as it would stop the horse from stepping under his weight into a square halt.

Inside and outside legs
In the following text you will sometimes see the expression 'outside leg' and 'inside leg'. This refers to the rider's legs. In this chapter there is a presumption made that you are either working your horse on a circle or in an arena or manege. The outside leg is the rider's leg nearest to the edge of the circle, arena or manege and the inside leg that nearest the middle of that area. If you were working on a clockwise circle or clockwise in an arena the right leg would be the inside leg and the left the outside leg. If you were working on an anticlockwise circle or anticlockwise in an arena the converse would be the case with the inside leg being the left leg and the outside leg the right leg. If you happened to be working in a straight line in an unenclosed area the expressions 'inside leg, outside leg' could not apply.

You will also see the expressions 'inside fore', 'inside hind', 'outside fore' and 'outside hind'. These are referring to the legs of the horse. The inside fore and hind are the front and back leg on the inside edge of the horse, or the side of the horse which is closest to the middle of the area you are working in. The outside fore and hind are the front and back legs of the horse which are on the side of the horse that is closest to the edge of the area you are working in.

Rising trot

Trot is a two-time motion in which the outside fore and the inside hind hit the ground at the same time as each other, as do the inside fore and the outside hind. So the rhythm is two-time, bump – bump, bump – bump, as each set of diagonals hit the ground. Notice in fig. 17 how each diagonally opposite pair of legs hits the ground at the same time.

If you were sitting to the trot you would sit at all times but when rising you will sit only as one pair of diagonals is touching the ground and rise out of the saddle as the other pair touches the ground. If you sit as the outside fore is on the ground you will also be sitting as the inside hind hits the ground or vice versa. The amount the rider lifts out of the saddle in rising trot should not be great or exaggerated in any way. The rider should use the movement of the horse to obtain lift from the saddle rather than putting any effort in to achieve any height above the saddle. This will mean that the amount of height gained by the rider will depend on the action of the horse.

The inside hind leg is the leg that does the most work in coming under the horse and supporting its weight. On your own feet run around in a clockwise circle. Can you feel the extra weight taken by your right leg? When the horse runs around in a circle his inside legs are taking most of the weight particularly the inside hind leg.

The main goal in our training of the horse is to make the hind legs stronger and come gradually further under the horse to support his weight better. By sitting as the inside hind leg hits the ground we are adding our weight to that of the extra weight already generated by the circling motion. This should make the inside hind leg even stronger. When we sit we can also use our back as a pushing aid. Sitting as the inside hind leg is used encourages the horse to push forward more with this hind leg and come further under the horse, carrying even more of the weight of the horse.

It is sometimes difficult to tell whether or not you are sitting on the correct diagonal at trot. Half close your eyes while you are trotting and concentrate your mind on the movement of the horse's legs. Try and feel it as each back leg comes underneath the horse and lifts him forwards. If

Fig. 17 The trot.

you know when each back leg is moving it shouldn't be too difficult to sit as the inside hind leg is stepping under you. If you find this difficult, lower your eyes (not your head) so that you can see the front of the horse's shoulders either side of his neck. As the horse trots, each front leg moves forwards alternately and at the same time each shoulder also moves forwards alternately. Hence you know that when the shoulder is moving forward, the leg underneath it is about to touch the ground. Because the outside fore and the inside hind hit the ground at the same time, if you sit as the outside front shoulder moves forwards you will be sitting as the inside hind leg is on the ground.

Basic aids

The aids are the system by which we communicate with the horse when we are riding. The tools we use to communicate these aids are the reins, our legs, our backs, the weight of our bodies or its displacement and our voice. These aids are virtually all man-made. Each of them has been devised as a way of letting the horse know what you want him to do. There are a few, particularly weight displacement aids, which do use the horse's natural reactions, but, other than this, the horse was not born with an awareness or knowledge of the aids and needs to be taught each of them.

We rarely use just one of these aids when we are riding and sometimes it will require the use of several at once to communicate exactly what is wanted. When we first use the aids with our horse we have to make them clearer by making them stronger. As the horse understands what we want we will gradually reduce its strength so that it is barely noticeable. The aids of a good horseman should be virtually undetectable by the onlooker, not just because it looks good, but because the less physical the aids the less disruption they make to the horse's fluency and rhythm.

Reins: With the reins we can turn the horse, slow the horse, stop the horse, harness the energy of the horse and/or support the horse.

Legs: With our legs we can ask the horse to move off,

increase speed or pace and ask him to step sideways to the right or to the left. We use our legs with the reins to bend the horse's body to the right or to the left, as when we turn a corner or go onto a small or large circle. Again with other aids, we use our legs when we ask the horse for a specific canter strike off or flying change and to make a downward transition. We also use our legs when we ask our horse to perform a rein back.

The legs should always have at least a gentle contact with the side of the horse. To apply the aid, the legs should increase the pressure by squeezing on the horse's flank either on the girth or just behind it, depending on which movement you require. The amount of pressure may vary depending on the horse's sensitivity to the leg and the movement. Ordinarily it should never be necessary to kick a horse. Sometimes a young or unschooled horse may require more pressure from your legs or perhaps even a gentle kick because the horse doesn't understand what you mean. As schooling progresses the kick should totally disappear and the pressure should become less and less as he becomes more and more aware and sensitised to the leg.

Backs: With our back we can either urge the horse forward by pushing down into the movement of the horse, or by bracing our back we can block the forward movement by no longer going with his rhythm.

Weight displacement: If we displace the weight of our bodies it means we have shifted our weight so that we are no longer in balance on the horse. He feels this imbalance. His reaction will be either to step in the direction of the imbalance to catch our weight, or to compensate by tensing muscles in his back. When we want the horse to perform lateral movements, putting more of our weight in the direction we wish him to step will help him understand what we want.

Voice: The voice is not a classical aid but one that can be a useful tool for soothing or encouraging the horse. The horse can also be taught to recognise some simple commands, though his recognition will be based more on the tone sequences than on the words themselves. For example: whenever you ask your horse to decrease speed, you would stretch the word of the command and probably lower your voice particularly on the second part of the word. Walk would become wa . . . alk, trot would be tro . . . ot, and halt would be ha . . . alt. If you want the horse to increase speed your tone would be totally different. Your voice would be higher pitched and you would further differentiate from the commands to reduce speed by adding another word such as 'on' and also by speaking briskly, rather than slowly. The command to walk from halt would then be 'walk on'. The command to trot would be 'trot on' and to canter merely 'canter' because this word has two syllables already. The voice is used more during the early days of training to help the horse understand the meaning of the other aids but as he begins to understand these the rider gradually dispenses with the voice.

When do we use what aids?

To increase speed: Both legs applied behind the girth gently or firmly depending on the amount of forward movement required or on the responsiveness of the horse. If the horse is already moving, the back can also be used to drive the horse forwards. When the horse is moving, the rider's body should move with and into the rhythm of the horse's movements. To use the back as a driving aid the rider sits deeper into the rhythm and accentuates it.

To reduce speed: The hands should be closed on the reins shortening the length of rein and strengthening the contact. The leg contact should be increased to ask the horse to step under himself so that the reduction of speed isn't lazy and energy is maintained despite the slower speed.

Upward transitions

To walk from halt: At halt you should maintain a contact with the horse's mouth. Do not allow the reins to loop or lose their tension. This contact should be maintained as the rider puts both legs just behind the girth. The horse should take a strong step with a hind leg whilst accepting the rein contact. He should not attempt to lift his head during the transition. If the rein contact was not maintained and the reins became loose the horse would stretch his head and neck and collapse forwards lazily onto his forehand as he moved into walk. Some horses will jog when they are supposed to be walking. Because they are going faster than you want them to it is a natural reaction to reduce the strength of the leg aid. In fact when a horse jogs rather than walks he is making life easier for himself. The short strides of jog are a lot easier for him than a proper stride at walk. So by jogging he is evading the rider's request to walk properly and swing his hind legs under his body. To insist that he do as we ask and use his hind legs better after we have persuaded him to return to walk we should put our legs on more strongly and push him into performing a correct walk. If the horse refuses to walk properly it helps if you increase the length of the rein and allow him to walk with a slightly stretched outline. In this shape he is more likely to remain in walk – it is easier for him than before. While keeping the legs on, gradually reduce the length of the rein until he is on the bit and walking in a shorter outline.

To trot: From halt or from walk the aids are the same. The contact should be maintained as both legs are applied behind the girth. The leg aid from halt to trot will be slightly stronger than the aid from walk to trot. The horse should remain on the bit during this transition and he should not be allowed to throw his head into the air.

The canter: A horse has two canters. One canter will have a right leading leg, the other a left leading leg. When a horse canters, his four legs work independently of each other. Most particularly you will notice the front two legs following a different pattern. One of his front legs will hit the ground a little in front of the other. It is called the leading leg. Watch a horse cantering – it is easy to spot the difference between the two legs. The horses in fig. 18 are

50

cantering on the left leading leg. You will notice that as the left foreleg comes to the ground it is more outstretched than the right foreleg and therefore lands further ahead of the right foreleg. This is shown in the upper drawing of fig. 18.

Leading leg

Fig. 18 The canter.

Cantering on a circle a horse will find it easier to canter with the inside fore leading. This is because, as when the horse was trotting in a circle, he has to put his inside hind leg well underneath him to carry his weight. Because the inside hind leg comes further forward so does the inside foreleg. It is this leg that we notice during the canter because it is easier to see, though in fact it is the hind leg coming further under the horse that is the reason this happens. Because this leg is in advance of the outside hind and comes further underneath the body of the horse, it will carry more weight of the horse and he will find it easier to balance himself.

Canter strike off, aids for correct canter: We need to be able to tell our horse which leg to lead with in canter, so that he will be more balanced when he canters. We ask for this when we ask the horse to canter (the strike off). To ask the horse to strike off with the inside leg leading, pivot your hips so that your inside shoulder is ahead of your outside shoulder and your inside hip ahead of your outside hip. This places more weight on your inside seat bone and consequently more weight on the horse's inside hind leg. It will make him want to strike off with the inside foreleg so that he better supports that extra weight.

Place your inside heel just behind the leg you wish the horse to strike off with, and place your outside leg just behind the girth. At the moment you wish the horse to strike off, both legs should increase their pressure. If the horse doesn't understand then increase the pressure even more with a gentle kick. Young or novice horses often get confused at the aids for the canter strike off and sometimes a lot of patience is needed. They will be helped to understand what you want them to do if you ask them to strike off at a corner or on a circle because this places even more weight on the inside hind leg of the horse. If the horse still has difficulty understanding which canter lead is required, tapping him on the inside shoulder at the moment of strike off may help him. It can take a while before a horse understands the aids for correct canter strike off so prepare to teach slowly and patiently if your horse is unsure.

It is often difficult to tell which leg the horse is leading with in canter. If you are not sure, look downward at the shoulders of the horse. Try not to tilt your head as you look as this may unbalance the horse. Instead look down with your eyes only. You will notice that as the horse canters the shoulders move slightly forward in the rhythm of the canter. You should also notice that one shoulder moves forwards just a little more than the other, this shoulder belongs to the leading leg. If this shoulder is the inside shoulder then your horse is leading with the correct leg.

Downward transitions

The hands should close on the reins so that the length of rein is shortened and the contact becomes stronger. At the same time the rider should brace his or her back, blocking the rhythm of the horse. The rider should also increase both leg aids in order to generate more energy from the hind legs so that they step well under the horse. These transitions should be forward going and energetic. The horse should not fall into the slower pace by gradually reducing speed. The second the horse has begun to make the transition, the back and stronger rein aid should cease whilst the leg aid should continue encouraging the horse to be forward going in this slower pace.

Transitions to halt: These aids are very similar to those required in all downward transitions. The horse should approach the halt in a forward going manner and he should be asked to step well under himself into the halt. The only difference in the aids to halt is that the rein aid is maintained for as long as the halt is required.

In halt all four legs should be at the corners of an oblong as in fig.19. (It is called a square halt –perhaps it should be called an oblong halt!) To perform it correctly the aids for a downward transition should be used. The hands should close on the reins and both legs should close around the horse. The back should be braced for the moment of transition, but no longer. The braced back discourages forward movement and, even though you want the horse to stop, just before he stops you want him to take a final step with his back legs bringing them well under him into the halt. Therefore the bracing of the back should cease the second you feel the horse drop out of the faster pace but the legs and hands should remain closed so that the horse

Fig. 19 Perhaps it should be called an oblong halt!

knows you want him to remain in halt. The action of the rider's legs should be sufficient to drive the horse into a square halt.

A correct halt will come to a horse so much more easily when he is balanced and ridden correctly into it. No matter how well you ride an unbalanced horse into a halt he will not necessarily achieve it. It will come when his work hits a level of balance where putting his back legs under him squarely comes almost naturally, not just on the odd occasion but every time. So don't worry about not getting square halts; only worry about achieving better balance. The halts will eventually look after themselves. In particular don't practise halts too often with your horse as this will tend to make him tense and the halts get worse and worse.

Rein back: Place both legs behind the girth as if you were asking the horse to move forwards. At the same time as you are applying pressure with your legs, your hands are closed around the reins saying no to any forward movement. The result should be a rein back. If the horse has never learnt these aids it may take a little while for him to understand what you want. A little gentle explanation in the form of someone on the ground may help. This person should stand facing the horse and push him backward with a hand on his chest at the same time as you give the aids.

To ride a bend or a circle
You should ask the horse to bend his body by bringing his head onto the track of the circle or bend with the inside rein. Your outside leg should be placed behind the girth to push the horse onto the track of the circle or bend. The outside rein checks the degree of bend and supports the inside rein (it stops the head coming in too far and the neck from bending too much). Increase the contact of the inside leg on the girth, keeping the middle section of the horse bent into the shape of the bend. As the size of the circle diminishes, the amount of bend asked for with the outside leg and the inside rein increases. The inside leg remains in the same place and becomes the pivot around which the horse bends. Fig. 20 explains this.

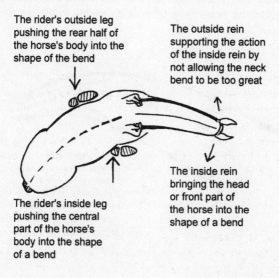

The rider's outside leg pushing the rear half of the horse's body into the shape of the bend

The outside rein supporting the action of the inside rein by not allowing the neck bend to be too great

The rider's inside leg pushing the central part of the horse's body into the shape of a bend

The inside rein bringing the head or front part of the horse into the shape of a bend

Fig. 20 Riding a circle or bend.

The inside rein should have a light, mobile contact. If you allowed this contact to be any stronger the horse would happily take it and use it for support. If he used it for support he would not need to step under his body to keep his balance – you would be giving him all the support he needed. He must always be encouraged to keep his own balance and not let you support him. If you had a strong contact with this rein, very soon you would find the horse leaning on your hand, particularly if this was his weaker rein. If the horse does this you will be aware of more weight in this rein than the outside rein and probably a tired and aching arm. If this is your problem read in Chapter 5, page 147, on how to ride a horse from the inside leg to the outside rein. The outside rein should maintain a stronger contact than the inside rein to catch the energy generated by the inside hind leg of the horse.

When working on a circle the horse bends his body to the shape of the circle. The measurement of the length of the outer, stretched side of his body will measure a lot more than the inner, squashed side of his body, as fig. 21 shows.

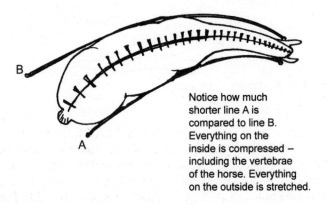

Notice how much shorter line A is compared to line B. Everything on the inside is compressed – including the vertebrae of the horse. Everything on the outside is stretched.

Fig. 21 The horse bends his body to the shape of the circle.

To accommodate this stretching and squashing, your outside hand should move forward allowing the outside edge of the horse to stretch and the inside hand should come backwards to indicate the amount of bend you require. Instead of thinking of this as two separate actions it is easier to keep your hands as they were when on a straight line. To turn the horse, rotate your body above your hips in the direction of the turn, keeping your arms and hands fixed in relation to your upper body. You will notice that the outside hand has advanced slightly along the neck of the horse, allowing it to stretch and lengthen. The inside hand has taken the inside rein slightly to the right of the withers, effectively shortening it and bringing the horse's head round in the direction you want to go, as shown in fig.22.

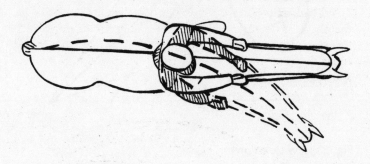

Fig. 22 Turning your horse.

There is perhaps some confusion about how much the rider's body needs to pivot. The official line has been that the rider's shoulders should be parallel to the horse's shoulders but if this were the case the body would have pivoted further than it should have. Look at fig. 23. The horse is bent on the curve of a circle. A line has been drawn through the horse's shoulders to the centre of the circle and also through the hips of the horse to the centre of the circle. A line drawn through the rider's body should also dissect the centre of the circle.

Look at the dotted line drawn that is parallel to the horse's shoulders. It does not dissect the centre of the circle, as it should have. A rider having pivoted as far as this line would be out of harmony with the horse.

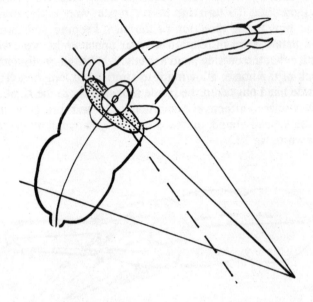

Fig. 23 How far to pivot.

Riding a circle in canter

When a horse is cantering he leads with his inside foreleg. This means that the inside of his body is a little ahead of the outside of his body and his inside shoulder is in front of his outside shoulder. A line drawn through the shoulders from outside to inside would no longer meet up with a line drawn through the quarters. Just as when riding a circle in walk and trot, the rider's shoulders should be in harmony with the horse's shoulders and the rider's inside shoulder should therefore be ahead of the outside shoulder. This will also put more weight over the rider's inside hip and therefore over the inside hind leg of the horse.

The whip

The whip is an extension of your leg aids. It is not designed for punishment but for communication between you and your horse. The horse should not fear the whip in any way though obviously he should listen to it and respect it. There are several types of whip including the lunge whip, the short jumping whip and the long schooling whip.

The *lunge whip* is approximately 2 metres (seven feet) long with a thong of similar length attached to the end of it. It is used to encourage the horse to work forwards when he is being lunged. By pointing it towards the horse's shoulder it can also be used to ask the horse to stay out on the circle and not turn towards the trainer. By placing it in front of the horse's line of sight it can also help the horse to understand when the trainer wishes him to slow or stop.

The short *jumping whip* is used behind the leg to reinforce the leg aid. If you felt the horse was not listening to your leg aids, a tap behind your leg would tell the horse to wake up and listen to what your leg was saying to him. An example would be where a horse is not going sufficiently forward as he approaches a jump. If he doesn't listen to the rider's leg, reinforcement with the whip should make him more aware of it. To use the whip like this it is necessary to put the reins in one hand and move the whip hand to behind the leg – this has the obvious disadvantages of interfering with the balance of the rider and hence the rhythm of the horse. This whip can also be used on the shoulder of the horse if he is running out at a jump. Held or tapped here it can help keep the horse on a straight approach to the jump.

Never ever use the whip when the horse is just about to take off or actually over the jump. It will totally disorient him physically and mentally. What would a horse hit like this think had been communicated by such a smack? I have no idea what the rider may have intended and I'm sure the horse would be even more confused. It would probably be a good way to put the horse off jumping if you punished him with a smack every time he took off.

The long *schooling whip* can be used while holding the reins and therefore shouldn't interfere with your balance or any other aspect of your riding. By using it just behind your leg it should make the horse listen to that leg even more than previously. You may want the horse to go away from your leg by moving sideways. If the stick was placed, tickled or tapped behind the leg that you wish him to go away from, the horse should realise that there was more power now to that leg. The stick is reinforcing the leg aid. It is almost as if the leg were stronger and therefore pushing harder than it was before.

Whether you merely hold it against the horse, tickle him with it or tap him with it will depend on your horse, his level of training and the amount of strength you wish to add to your leg aid. Some horses respond more to a tickle or a tap than they do a whack with the stick. You may imagine that a horse would hardly feel a tickle but think how quickly the horse notices the presence of flies. He always manages to feel and respond to them!

The long schooling whip would also be used to exaggerate the leg aid if you wanted the horse to work more energetically. If he wasn't listening to your legs when you asked for more impulsion or wasn't responding to your leg aids in a transition you would use the schooling whip behind your leg to emphasise and increase the aid, as shown in fig. 24.

It is normal to hold your whip in your inside hand because the inside hind leg of the horse is the leg we wish to stimulate to work harder and therefore the whip is in the correct position to use if you need it. Sometimes you might put your whip in your outside hand if the horse isn't bending his body to the shape of the circle or bend you are working him on. He is bending his neck but not his body – from his shoulders to his quarters he is straight. To the onlooker this looks as if his quarters are swinging out of the circle. When a horse does this it is described as falling out through the quarters. If your horse did this you would increase your outside leg aid and would also hold the whip against his side behind your outside leg. Doing this should reinforce the leg when it asks him to bend his body into the shape of the bend or circle. Fig. 25 shows how to do this.

As with all other aids it is the aim of the good rider to gradually reduce them and make them as indiscernible to the onlooker as possible. This is not for the sake of the

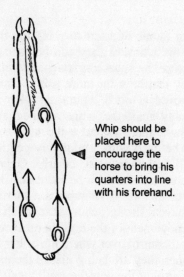

Whip should be placed here to encourage the horse to bring his quarters into line with his forehand.

Fig. 24 The long schooling whip.

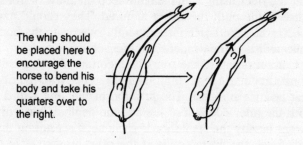

The whip should be placed here to encourage the horse to bend his body and take his quarters over to the right.

Fig. 25 To prevent the horse from falling out through the quarters.

onlooker. If the aids are minimised they will require less movement of the rider and hence less interference with the horse's performance.

The spurs

The spurs can either be used to reinforce the rider's leg aids, as with the whip, or they can be used to clarify the leg aids. Because the spurs are attached to both of the rider's heels they can be a lot more useful than the whip as both can be used at once. Spurs can also be used with greater accuracy than the whip as they are applied at virtually the same place as and at the same time as the leg. Spurs should be used with a relatively gentle pressure, as the horse will feel them very clearly. Only if the horse ignores this pressure should it be increased. Because spurs are attached to the leg it is important that anyone using them should have a strong, secure seat which allows totally independent movement of the legs. In other words the rider must have total control over where his or her legs are being placed and when they are being placed there. If a rider has inadequate control of the legs they will inevitably touch the horse's side with the spurs when it isn't intended and because the spurs have such a strong action they will give the horse a very definite incorrect message. It is important that the rider using spurs should keep them away from the horse's side until the aid is required. They should not be used to nag the horse intermittently otherwise the horse's sides will become deadened to their effect.

Correct fitting of the spurs is important if they are to be of maximum use with minimal interference with the rider's seat and leg position. The position of the spur will differ with the rider's length of leg and the depth of girth of the horse. Ideally the spur should sit in such a position that it will touch the horse's side if the rider brings the heel in towards the horse. It is not desirable for the rider to have to lift the leg up or back so that the spur can connect. Such a lot of movement by the lower leg may confuse the horse and probably interfere with the rider's balance. When contact with the spur is not required the rider should hold the foot parallel to the horse's side so that the leg but not the spur is touching the horse.

If a horse has never felt spurs before it is advisable to minimise the possible shock felt by him by gently pressing them against his sides behind the girth while dismounted.

Do this on several occasions before you wear them while riding. Letting him feel them first allows you to make sure they do not cause him any great concern and also helps him get used to them before you take the risk of using them while mounted.

LATERAL AIDS

Moving away from your leg

Teaching the horse to move away from your leg is a very basic part of equitation and a lesson he should learn earlier rather than later. Prepare him to understand what you are going to ask him by pushing him with your hand when you are unmounted. You can practise in the stable by putting your hand against his flanks and asking him to move away from it. Don't be surprised if at first he leans on you when you try to push him over. It will not be long before he realises what you mean. Later you will be able to substitute your hand with your leg to push him over when you are mounted. It will help the horse to understand what is required if someone on the ground was to push him sideways at the same time as you put your leg on. There is more about this in Chapter 5, page 161 onwards.

Because it is not physically difficult for the young or unschooled horse, and because it is an important lesson for the horse to learn, there are no physical reasons why he shouldn't learn it as soon as training starts. A schooled horse should be listening at all times to the lateral aids given by the legs so that he knows what shape to bend his body in and where to put his back legs.

Corridor of power

Your reins guide the front end of the horse. Your legs control the rest of the horse. Together they are capable of controlling all the movement of the horse. It is described as being between hand and leg. The horse's body sits between your legs. The legs not only drive forwards but also control the bend and direction of the horse from behind the withers. Your hands are controlling the speed that the energy produces and also directing where the front of the horse goes. Both of them together should control the shape and direction of every part of the horse as he moves.

Our reins need to be constantly in contact with the mouth of the horse, giving him instructions on direction and speed. In the same way our legs should be constantly in contact with the sides of our horse to let him know what shape we want his body to be and how much energy we want him to generate with his back legs. If they are not asking him to generate much energy then the contact will be light. If you wish him to increase the amount of energy or increase the amount of bend then you should increase the amount of contact. He needs to know you are there all the time ready to tell him what he is doing next or he will be wondering if the next decision should be his.

Obedience to the leg
The horse needs to listen to your leg aids and obey them willingly and immediately. If you use a leg aid to ask the horse to go faster or go into another pace he should not need to be asked twice to do as you ask. He should give you exactly what you want and when you want it. Some horses will wait to be asked two or three times before they work properly and very often the rider has to use the aids much more strongly than is desirable to get the horse to be obedient. Curing this situation is only a matter of training. If you think your horse is not going to obey you immediately use a stronger aid initially. If this doesn't work use a stick to reinforce your aid. A long schooling stick tapping your horse just behind your leg should suffice. You have to let your horse know you mean business and have to insist that you are obeyed every time. It is only when the horse has accepted that he has to obey you that you can begin to reduce the aids.

If the horse is lazy he probably finds it hard to work energetically and when you put your leg on he will try to ignore it. You must work hard to insist that he listens to your leg and uses as much energy as you want him to. If he is always worked forwards energetically and he is always made to listen to and obey your leg aids, gradually he will become more forward going. In other words by always riding your horse forwards energetically you can sometimes turn a sluggish horse into a forward going horse. Until you succeed in making him listen and obey your leg aids, he is making the decisions as to what speed he goes at or how much energy he uses – perhaps without your knowing it he is also making other decisions that you should be making. Indiscipline is rarely confined to one area. When you are riding you must always be the one to decide what he will do, when he will do it and in what manner.

With horses that are naturally forward going there is a different problem. You may feel that there is no reason to ask the horse to work more energetically because he is already going in the manner you want him to of his own free will. You may feel he is listening to your leg aids because he is so forward going but in fact this horse could also be making the decisions as to what energy he produces. You need to know that you are truly in control of all aspects of your horse's way of going so that if a difference is required he will know to obey it. Keeping him listening to your leg aids is essential; if you ask for more energy he must give it to you even if he is already working forwards. It is most important that your horse knows and accepts that you are in control. Have you ever seen a horse careering around a show jumping course or a cross-country course at an incredible rate of knots only to stop at the next fence? There will be other reasons, of course, but one of the main reasons the horse has stopped is because it was not listening to the rider's leg aids. It was going with a lot of energy, and speed, but it was doing it because it wanted to and not because of the rider's commands. When the rider put the leg on and asked the horse to jump he happily ignored the rider's wishes because in the horse's head he was the one in charge of forward movement!

3

On the Bit – What It Means and How to Achieve It

What is on the bit?

When the horse is on the bit the horse's head is at such an angle that the bit is able to lie on the bars of his mouth. From this position the reins should run in a straight line from there to the rider's hands. The bars of the horse's mouth are situated on the lower jaw above the semicircle of incisors and beneath the front molars. Here there is a wide gap on either side of the jaw in which there are no teeth. The bit is designed to lie on these bars. They are shown in fig. 26.

When a horse comes on the bit he relaxes and stretches the muscles along the top line of the neck and relaxes his jaw. This action should put the head of the horse in the right position to be on the bit. Look at fig. 27. See the upper horse. His neck is straight and his nose is poking forwards. You would describe him as being above the bit, a position which most untrained horses like to adopt. You can see that the bit cannot lie properly on the bars because of the angle of the reins coming from the rider's hands. It would most likely lie against the corner of the lower molars or on top of the molars. The rider would have to lower his hands down the shoulder of the horse for the bit to lie against the bars. Look now at the lower horse. This horse has stretched the top outside edge of his neck and slightly lowered his head. His nose no longer points forwards – it points downwards and you can see

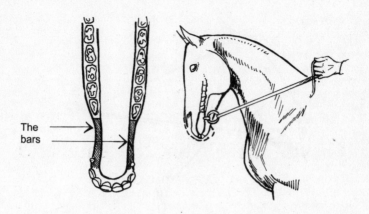

Fig. 26 The bars.

that the bit would now lie on the bars.

In the upper horse you can see the resistance of the horse's neck. He has set it straight and rigid and he may well be holding the bit between his teeth so that he won't feel the effect of it on his bars. Because his jaw is so strong he will be able to put his head at this angle and completely ignore your rein aids. The resistance and tension that you see in this horse's neck will continue down through his back making it impossible for him to relax and round his back and work properly. In effect the whole of his body has been braced and set against you.

Notice how much greater the distance is on the top edge of the neck of the horse that is on the bit than of the top edge of the neck of the horse that is not. Notice also how much shorter the distance is on the underneath of the neck of the horse that is on the bit than is on the underneath of the neck of the other. It shows how much the horse has to stretch the top line of his neck and how much he has to compress the under side of his neck to be on the bit.

The horse has rounded his neck and relaxed his jaw becoming softly accepting of the contact and control of the

67

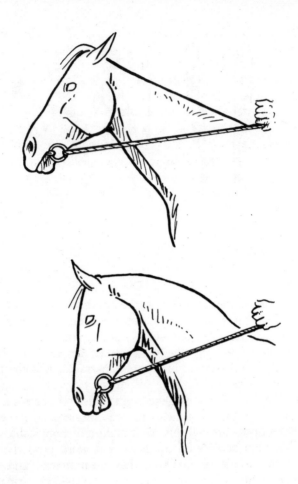

Fig. 27
(Top) Above the bit.
(Below) On the bit.

bit. You can feel the change come about when the horse does this. The horse relaxes his pull on the bit as if he is accepting your control of him. This changes the feel of the reins in your hands – you still have a contact but it is lighter. Despite its lightness you know that the horse is under your control and listening to you. He is now willingly submitting himself to your control rather than grudgingly. So, even though there is a very physical side to the horse being on the bit, the most important aspect of being on the bit is the mental submission of the horse when he allows you to control him.

It is important that in your efforts to get the horse on the bit you do not force his head and neck into a restricted position. The neck should always remain stretched and rounded and not squashed and short. It should appear to grow out of the shoulders, not as if it had been stuck onto them.

WHAT IS THE EFFECT OF THE HORSE BEING ON THE BIT?

1. Opposing directional forces

When the horse is on the bit he is accepting your control of the speed at which he goes. It is possible for you now to drive the horse forwards, with your leg and seat aids, and at the same time slow him up with your rein aids. Your legs are asking for the power from the hind legs and your hands are controlling the length of stride of the front legs. The result should be a horse that is working energetically with his back legs but still not going fast. The power has been harnessed by the reins converting it into energy rather than speed. His frame should shorten and his strides should become more elevated. A horse ridden like this is often likened to a spring that is being pushed together. The more you push the two ends of the spring together, the more energy you are harnessing in the coiled steel.

We are able to harness this power because the horse submits his will to our control and also because of the physical laws that govern his movement. Because of the angle of the horse's head, the directional force of the reins is directly backwards and immediately opposite to the directional force of the energy generated by the hind legs. These opposing directional energies, shown in fig. 28, are the physical means by which we harness the power of the horse.

Fig. 28 Opposing directional forces.

2. The shape of the horse's spine

When the horse relaxes and stretches his neck to come on
the bit he also has to bend and stretch his back in the same
way. Being on the bit encourages the horse to round his
back properly and helps him to be in a position where he is
able to put his back legs underneath him (fig. 29B). Some
horses are weak in the back and cannot cope with the strain
that being on the bit and rounding their spines puts on their
back muscles. In this case they will resist being on the bit
and often hollow their backs (fig. 29A).

Notice how your horse holds his tail. Because it is a
continuation of the spine it can tell you a fair amount about
the shape of his back. If it is sticking up high in the air, the
back is probably hollowed. If the tail is held at an odd
angle, there may well be something wrong with the spine
of the horse.

The stretchy top line

In fig. 29 there are two horses. The spine of horse A is
concave. The spine of horse B is convex, as it should be. If
you were to measure the length of the spine in example A
(the concave spine) and also measure the length of the

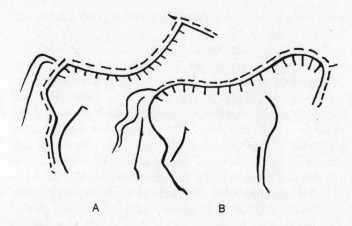

Fig. 29
A Hollowed back.
B Back rounded properly.

spine in example B (the convex spine) you would find that spine B is considerably longer than A even though it is the same spine. Spine A is squashed together whereas the convex spine is stretched and consequently measures more.

When you work a horse, envisage this imaginary line drawn from the nose to the poll along the neck and back and then down the back legs of the horse. I think of it as a stretchy top line though in truth it isn't really that stretchy but stretch is what we want it to do. We need to make it become as long as possible. Using exercises which will make it stretch in different places such as the neck, the back or the legs will make the horse more supple along this top line allowing the horse to step further under him and carry more of his weight with his hind legs.

An apt comparison with the human frame would be the suppleness of our own spine. If you touch your toes with your fingers you can feel the back of your legs stretch and probably hurt – depending on your suppleness. If you touched your toes every day and pushed the limits of your ability to stretch, soon you would do it with ease. This is what we are going to persuade the horse to do – not touch his toes – stretch his spine!

We first help the horse to stretch his spine when we ask him to work on the bit. This particularly stretches the front part of the spine – the neck – but it does stretch the whole of the spine at the same time. After this the exercises mostly involve movements which encourage the horse to step further under him so that he is stretching the back part of his spine and his back legs. Stretching any one part of the line more than it is usually stretched will affect all of the rest of the line and make it feel that it too is being stretched. You may see the horse experience this when you ask for a transition, particularly into canter. The horse may be going nicely but at the time of the transition he will want to lift his head in the air. This is because if the transition is executed properly it will have stretched part of the top line (that bit that wraps around his quarters and goes down his legs) as the horse steps under his weight. If he is insufficiently supple along his top line he will lift his head in the air to release one part of the line, i.e. the front part, so that he is freer to stretch another part, i.e. the part that runs between his quarters and his hocks.

If you ask the horse to be more forward going you will also be stretching the top line. This is because when the horse is more forward going he has to put his hocks further under him. If a horse is on the bit but only just able to cope with the stretching this requires, he will find it much easier when the pace is slow. Working on the bit at walk will be easy. If he is asked to be more forward going in walk he will find it more difficult to stay on the bit because the extra forward movement is making his hocks go further under him. You are stretching that top line at the back as well as the front. If you then ask for trot, as long as the trot is forward going, it will stretch the line even further. At canter it is even more so. This is particularly the case if your horse is jumping. He really has to put his hocks under him to lift his weight off the ground and unless he is very supple along his top line he will need a lot of freedom with his head and neck to take off.

WHAT IS BEHIND THE BIT?

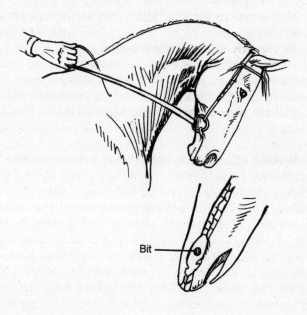

Fig. 30 Behind the bit.

When the horse is behind the bit he pulls his head into his chest as in fig. 30. The front of his face is behind the vertical. This is because he doesn't want the bit to lie on the bars. When he brings his head closer to his chest he is pulling the bars away from a contact with the bit. The bit then hangs in the gap between the jaws. Looking at the horse from the side it appears that the bit is lying on the bars of the mouth *but* in fact the horse is stopping the bit from touching the bars by drawing his head back to his chest. Every time the rider shortens the reins to find a contact with the bars the horse will draw his chin back even further.

What is the cause of the horse being behind the bit?

1. He doesn't want you to have control.
2. The bars in his mouth are narrow or have very little flesh on them which makes the bit hurt.
3. He has previously been ridden with harsh hands and/or a harsh bit.
4. He has been ridden in tight running reins.
5. He has a tush tooth (a small extra tooth growing on the lower bars or above the bars) or mouth ulcers or sores.
6. He has a weak neck or back and isn't strong enough to lift his head high enough to take a good contact with the bit.

What is the effect of the horse being behind the bit?

Because the horse refuses to take a contact he is either avoiding the feel of the bit on the bars of the mouth or avoiding your control. Because you have no contact you are not able to ask him to slow or stop effectively and have no means of harnessing the power of his hind legs. When the horse is behind the bit he lowers his head, as in fig. 31, so that the poll is no longer the highest point and the face of the head becomes behind the vertical. In this situation we are lacking the two essential ingredients we need for harnessing the energy of the horse: firstly the submission of the horse's will to our control and secondly the physical control of the opposing directional forces.

The directional force of the reins needs to be opposite to the directional power of the hind legs if it is to be effective in harnessing and controlling it. When the horse is behind the bit the directional force of the reins is no longer backwards but upwards and out through the withers, in other words lost and ineffective.

The other effect of being behind the bit is that the horse is holding himself in an unnatural position to avoid the action of the bit. His neck and the rest of his frame are rather squashed and in this position it is not possible for him to use himself as well as he could. He is pinning himself in an uncomfortable position that doesn't allow him free use of his body.

Fig. 31 Behind the bit: no means of harnessing the power of his hind legs.

How to stop the horse being behind the bit

Pain inflicted by the bit is most often the cause of a horse being behind the bit. The most obvious solution, if this is the case, is to remove the cause of the pain, i.e. ride with softer hands if they are too harsh, or put a fatter bit in the horse's mouth if a narrow bit has hurt him. In the case of a tush tooth your vet will be able to remove it for you without a great deal of fuss or pain. In the case of mouth ulcers or sores do not ride him until they have healed. Do not expect him to improve immediately because he will almost certainly remember the pain the bit has caused in the past and it will take him a while to realise that the new bit and/or the soft hands no longer cause him any pain. At the same time ride him forward energetically to encourage him to stretch his neck and the rest of his frame.

Take hardly any contact at first but when his frame has stretched its outline try a gentle contact with the bit. Don't be surprised if he draws backwards from it and comes behind the bit again as this may be the first time he has properly felt the bit since it used to hurt him. Lessen the contact and later increase it gradually. Eventually he should realise it won't hurt him. It is most important you always ride him forwards energetically while you are trying to get him to accept a contact so that he learns to stretch his head and neck and use the whole of his body in a relaxed, fluid way.

When a horse is behind the bit his poll is not the highest point because he has to lower his head to bring his chin back towards his chest. It may be possible for you to persuade the horse to lift his head by lifting your hands up in the air and thereby putting pressure on the corners of the mouth in an upward direction. To relieve this pressure the horse should lift his head. This lifting of the head would mean he was no longer behind the bit. It should not be maintained for longer than a second or two nor should it be in any way harsh. Gentle occasional lifts will let him know what you want. If he is prepared to oblige, you won't have to do this for long. Never let the lift degenerate into a pull – always keep it light and gentle. If and when he does lift his head remember to keep the contact as light as possible so that he won't have any reason to go behind the bit again.

Because a horse that is behind the bit refuses to let you use the reins as a means of stopping or slowing him it is useful if you can put extra effort into training him to obey your leg and back aids to slow or stop. You may still use the reins to a degree but if he can become obedient to the other stopping or slowing aids you will be able to keep the rein aids to the very minimum.

If the reason the horse is coming behind the bit is because he has discovered it is a way to evade your aids the solution should be the same. Drive the horse forward with little contact to encourage him to stretch his frame. You will probably have to do this for some time before the horse changes his way of going and lengthens his outline. If the horse has a tendency to tank off with you then it would probably be advisable to do this work in some kind of enclosed area. Again teach your horse to slow or stop using a light rein aid combined with more effective seat and leg aids.

The horse may have a weak back or neck and this may prevent him from lifting his head and taking a good contact with the bit. This is often the case with a young or novice horse and is corrected over the course of time by exercises which strengthen his back and neck.

WHAT IS ABOVE THE BIT?

When the horse is above the bit his head is at such a high angle that the bit does not lie on the bars of his mouth. If the horse's mouth and teeth are closed, the bit will lie against the closed teeth, as in fig. 32 (top), or the horse may have lifted the bit with his tongue onto the top of the front premolars where he will grasp it between the upper and lower sets of teeth, as in fig. 32 (bottom). If the bit is between his teeth the horse is able to use his great strength to hold the bit there and stop the rider from having any control of him. If the horse's mouth is open, the bit will slide between the upper and lower sets of teeth and will pull against the corners of the mouth. If this happens, the bit will make the horse want to lift his head even higher in the air away from the pressure on the corners of his mouth.

What are the causes of the horse being above the bit?

If you watch the horse running around on his own without a rider on board he will always push his nose out in front of him looking just the same as a horse that is above the bit. It is the horse's natural way of going. When you ride him it is natural for him to adopt the same position. To ask a horse to relax his jaw and go onto the bit puts him in an unnatural position and therefore one that you will have to teach him. Because it is not natural he will probably also find it at least a little difficult to achieve and to maintain. The physical difficulty will depend on his natural conformation. The mental difficulty will depend on how well you teach him what you want. The following are some of the reasons why the horse doesn't come onto the bit:

1.   The rider's rein aids are not asking enough of the horse.
2.   His back or neck is stiff, weak or injured and he,

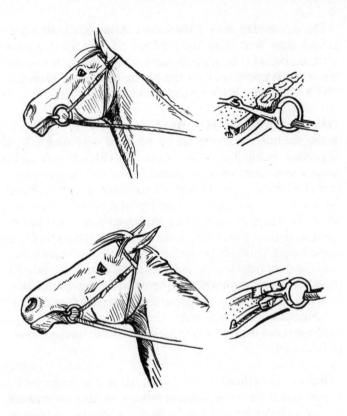

Fig. 32 Above the bit:
(Top) the bit lies against the closed teeth
(Bottom) the bit is grasped between the teeth.

therefore, finds it physically difficult to round his neck/
back. If he cannot round his back he cannot round his neck
and go onto the bit.

3.   The horse hardly feels the pressure of the bit because
the bars in his mouth are wide or fleshy, making the
pressure of the bit too greatly spread for him to feel it and
"listen" to your hands. If the bit were thick this may have
the same effect. It is also possible that the horse's tongue is
fat and wide and overlaps the bars when the bit presses
down on it putting the tongue between the bit and the bars.

4. The muscles under his neck are too well developed and there is too much bulky tissue there. When the horse goes onto the bit he needs to stretch the top line of his neck and at the same time compress the underside of his neck. If there is too much muscle underneath his neck it can be difficult for him to do this.

5. The rider is coming down too heavily on the horse's back making the horse brace his back against the pain. If the horse braces his back it cannot be relaxed or rounded and he cannot come onto the bit.

6. He doesn't want to work as hard as you want him to or he wishes to evade your control.

7. The horse does not like the nutcracker effect of the single jointed snaffle bit – either it hurts his bars or the joint may be hitting the roof of his mouth.

What is the effect of the horse being above the bit?

1. His back is bent in totally the wrong shape for correct work to begin. His legs cannot begin to come under him to improve his balance. See fig. 33.

Compare this with a horse whose back is correctly rounded, as in fig. 34.

The shape of his back allows his hind legs the freedom to come well under him.

2. The rider has reduced control through the reins of the horse.

3. The horse has not submitted himself to your control. He is still fighting to be in charge.

4. There is no opposing directional force.

How to stop the horse being above the bit

Before you start to solve the problem of your horse being above the bit, remember that you should always aim for his poll being the highest point, with the face of the horse not coming behind the vertical. It should be as shown in fig. 28.

Fig. 33 His back is bent in totally the wrong shape.

Fig. 34 His back is correctly rounded.

It is also very important that when the horse comes onto the bit he drops onto it by stretching and rounding his neck as well as relaxing his jaw. If he is made to come on the bit by merely pulling his jaw backwards you will have squashed and stiffened the neck rather than having stretched and rounded it. The horse will be pinned into position and hence restricted by the reins rather than merely controlled by them. If he is pinned down by the reins it will make him much less athletic and the stiffness that has been created in the neck will affect the whole of his body. He has to have free use of his neck for him to use his body properly. Imagine how you would feel if asked to, say, dance while your chin was tied down to your chest. You wouldn't be able to move very gracefully!

Methods such as running reins or possibly even very harsh hands will have this effect on the neck of the horse. There are even some trainers who attach very short side reins to their horses, pinning their heads onto the bit and leaving them in the stable for hours on end to get them to go on the bit. These horses must go through agony being held down like this and all to no avail. The neck is being compressed rather than stretched and when released from the contraption, even if it stays in that fixed shape, it would be much less athletic and supple than it should be. Some people get their horses to come onto the bit by see-sawing the reins. They will pull on the right rein and then the left rein alternately until the horse decides to get away from the grating action of the bit by coming behind it. Always resist the temptation to do this. Although it often will make the horse drop onto the bit it frequently results in a horse that develops a habit of dipping his head back and forth at all times even when the rider isn't see-sawing the reins.

1. Rein aids

If your rein aids are weak and ineffectual or your reins too long the horse will have no reason to come on the bit – you haven't actually asked him to.

Shorten the reins until you can feel the horse's mouth on the other end but without pulling on the reins. At first do this while your horse is standing still. Next shorten the reins just a little bit more. If the horse knows how to come onto the bit he should just nod his head and gently drop onto it. If he doesn't know what you mean, lower your hands down the shoulders/neck of the horse so that the bit lies square on the bars and through the reins you have a direct contact with them. Gently, with a giving and taking movement, ask him to relax his jaw and lower his head – it is much easier for him to know what you want if you actually show him. He should come down onto the bit fairly easily – then perhaps you will be lucky and he will remain like that when your hands are in the normal position. It is not your intention to yank the horse onto the bit or even to force him into this position – more to show him what you want by saying to him, ''here are my hands – relax your neck and head and drop onto them – don't fight them''. There is more information on rein aids in Chapter 2.

When the horse first comes onto the bit he may find it difficult. If this is true do not ask too much of him at first, either in length of lesson or difficulty in work. Walk at first and then trot. Rise in the trot and land in the saddle with a soft, supple back. Initially don't ask for too much forward propulsion as being on the bit stretches the top line. When the horse goes faster this stretches the top line even more and may make it harder for the horse. If his first associations with being on the bit are unstressed and favourable, hopefully he will always be happy to come on the bit.

If you are working a young horse whose muscles are not yet sufficiently developed, ask him to come onto the bit with a longer length of neck than you would expect of an older, better developed horse.

2. A weak, sore or stiff back

A horse has to round his neck and back when he works on the bit and this stretches the whole of the top line. This includes the ligaments and muscles that are behind the saddle and in the quarters and hind leg of the horse. If any of these muscles are stiff and/or weak the horse will find the stretching (that being on the bit requires) difficult and possibly painful. Naturally he will fight your efforts to make him work on the bit. He may put his head in the air and hollow his back to relieve the strain that rounding the back and stepping underneath him will cause. It is essential that you have sympathy with this horse and only ask him to work on the bit for relatively short periods of time. He would benefit even more from a period of work on the lunge. The mere action of being on a circle will make his inside hind leg step further underneath him and hence begin to stretch and strengthen his back.

Strongly built, muscular horses tend to have more of a problem relaxing onto the bit than do slim, lithe horses. This is because there is such a bulk of muscle and body tissue it holds itself together in a relatively fixed position. Have you ever seen a boxer's arms that are so packed with muscle they cannot stretch out straight and so they are limited in the distance that his arm can reach? They are muscle-bound. Horses packed with muscle or other dense tissue are very similar and therefore can find it difficult to stretch their bodies either along their top line or along both lateral lines. Their advantage is that when they come to do work which needs muscle strength they have more than their more delicately built friends. Lithe horses rarely have any difficulty in stretching their bodies to get onto the bit but they will have problems with work that requires strength and muscle power.

If the horse does not easily or willingly come onto the bit, it is possible he may be experiencing pain there. If the horse's tail carriage is stiff it may indicate a problem in the back. Whether this is the case or not it may be a good idea to have his back checked by a horse back specialist. If there is something wrong this could be the reason your horse is unhappy about coming on the bit.

3.   Softness of the rider's back
Sit as softly in the saddle as you can. The effect of a rider landing hard on the horse's back will not be conducive to a horse rounding his back. It is a little like someone about to take a punch at your stomach. Because you know the blow is coming you will tense the muscles in your stomach to minimise the hurt. If the horse is expecting a thud from the

weight of his rider he will do the same with his back muscles. He will tense them and hold his back rigid. We want him to relax and stretch his back. The neck is continuation of the back and so if the back isn't rounded neither can the neck be rounded and the horse cannot relax his jaw and come onto the bit. This is why it is especially important to ride with a supple back and particularly true at trot where you can ride either sitting with a back that absorbs the bouncing of the movement or rising when the rider must make a soft contact with the saddle when he sits.

4. Is the bit correct?

Read through Chapter 4, on bits and how they work, to see if you have got the correct bit in the horse's mouth. It is quite possible that your bit is too fat and the horse hardly feels it against his bars and therefore doesn't respect it at all. In this case you may need a narrower bit. Perhaps the tongue is too large and insensitive and when the bit presses down towards the bars the tongue gets in the way and stops the bars from getting any pressure. It could be that the bars are fleshy and wide so that the bit, despite its narrowness, is barely felt and certainly not respected by the horse. If your horse has a mouth like this it may be necessary to teach him to respect the bit by using one with a more severe action. In a normal snaffle he may only be on the bit if it suits him and if the work gets hard it probably won't suit him.

If the horse is constantly refusing your requests to come on the bit, and you have eliminated all other reasons for his disobedience, you will have to try a stronger bit. Otherwise both you and the horse will expend unnecessary energy fighting each other, and the horse will remain on the forehand throughout, never working properly. A double bridle could be tried or a Pelham with two reins. Both of these have a similar action and both require the accurate and sympathetic riding of an experienced rider – all of which is described in the next chapter. When a stronger bit is used correctly the horse should say "O.K. I give in now – I'll do what you want". Because he knows you are stronger and because it will hurt him if he fights you, the horse often doesn't even try to disobey you. He uses half as much energy doing as you ask than he did before in fighting you. Previously you were both exhausted and had achieved little. Now you both have energy to spare. The horse becomes light and responsive and you can direct his energy into where it will be most useful. Because the bit is stronger the rider's use of it must be much more sensitive and as soon as the horse accedes to the rider's wishes the rider must reward the horse with a lighter, softer contact.

It may only be necessary to use the above when you are teaching your horse something that is more difficult and which requires greater effort from him. If you are asking the horse to bring his hocks further under him you are stretching the top line more. The horse may well try to take the easy way out and lift his head. Doing this will make it very easy for the horse to perform; it will unfortunately make the exercise useless. You need to be able to dissuade him from this and tell him you want him to stay on the bit even though it is a little difficult for him. After he has achieved what you want with ease, you should be able to return to your normal bit. If there is a chance that your horse dislikes the feel of the nutcracker effect of a single jointed snaffle try him in a French link. This bit softly follows the contours of the horse's tongue/bars without any nutcracker action.

5. The horse with the bit between his teeth

If you describe a person as having the bit between the teeth it means he or she really means business – whatever this person is going to do, it will be done with determination. When a horse gets the bit between his teeth he really means business. That's where the bit is and that's where he intends to keep it. While it is there no one can make him do what they want – he is in charge. As described earlier he will have his head quite high with his nose pointing forwards and no amount of pulling on the reins will make him slow up or drop onto the bit if he doesn't want to. You could try a Pelham or double bridle on this horse. Either bit will help you to match his strength and determination. A bubble bit (Continental or Dutch Gag) would also give you more control of the horse while he holds it between his teeth.

6. Muscle under the neck

Quite a few horses find the rounding of the neck and back difficult because nature has given them a mass of muscle underneath the neck. As they relax and stretch the top of their necks they need to squash up the underside of the neck. If there is too much firm tissue there it makes this difficult for them to do. See fig. 35. This is more often a problem with older horses who are more likely to have strong muscle than younger horses.

Obviously these horses would have great difficulty bending their necks. The fitter the horse, the more muscle will be there and the greater difficulty the horse will have in coming onto the bit. The more unfit the horse, the flabbier and softer the muscle tissue and the easier it will be to compress it. Start work on these horses when they are unfit, perhaps in the middle of winter and on a low ration or even better when they are young and relatively supple. Working on the lunge with side reins would be a good way to try and change their shape. You can expect to be doing this work for some time before you will see much change in their musculature and it becomes easier for them to come onto the bit.

7. Teeth or salivary gland problems

If you have not recently had your horse's teeth checked, now would be a good time to do so. He may have a tush tooth, as in fig. 36, that would make the bit lying on the bars uncomfortable.

It is also possible that the teeth may have become sharp on the outside edge. This would cause pain when the cheek pieces or rings of the bit push the flesh of the cheek onto the sharp tooth. Fig. 37 shows the kind of thing that can be a problem.

If your horse had ulcers in his mouth this could cause the bit to hurt him which would lead him to resenting it and trying to evade contact with it.

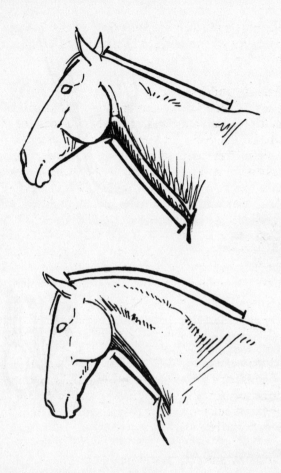

Fig. 35 The horse can have difficulty in coming on to the bit if he has a lot of tissue and muscle under the neck.

Blocked salivary gland

Occasionally it is possible for a horse to suffer from a blocked or inflamed salivary gland. As these glands sit behind the jaw of the horse, flexing it to come onto the bit may be difficult for him.

When a horse works on the bit the relaxing of the jaw should stimulate the production of saliva that helps the

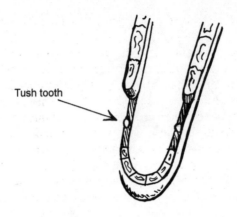

Tush tooth

Fig. 36 Tush teeth.

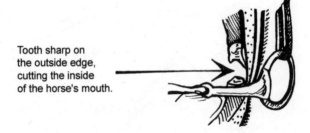

Tooth sharp on
the outside edge,
cutting the inside
of the horse's mouth.

Fig. 37 Sharp tooth edge.

horse mouth the bit – if there is a problem with the salivary
glands this does not happen and the horse has a dry mouth.
If everything is well with the glands when on the bit the
horse should produce some saliva which shows itself as
white froth in the horse's mouth when the horse is working. Sometimes there is so much it comes out of the mouth
and drips to the ground. Its presence, therefore, whether a
little or a lot, is a good sign. If the horse does not produce
saliva it does not necessarily mean there is a problem with
the glands but it may alert you to this possibility.

The salivary glands are around the back of the cheekbone and under the jaw. If there is a blockage you should feel a thickness or puffiness behind the cheekbone or under the jaw. It would normally only affect one side of the jaw. It is easy to imagine that flexing his jaw and compressing the underside of his neck would be difficult with any thickness there. Run your hands around the cheekbones as shown in fig. 38, starting at the higher point just under the ears and coming down under the bone and then under the jaw. If you feel there is thickness or puffiness run your fingers down this line. If you find it, gently massage the area to help move the blockage. If you think there may be a problem here it may be worth asking your vet or horse dentist to have a look.

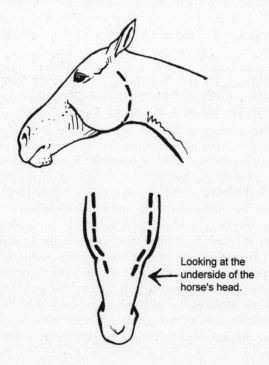

Looking at the underside of the horse's head.

Fig. 38 Run your hands around and under the cheekbone.

Jumping

A horse that is on the bit and whose back is rounded and supple will jump better than a horse that is not in the correct shape. This is because he is so much more supple and athletic and the improvement in his balance will help him to attain even more height over the jump. A horse going correctly is also a lot easier to ride, steer and control than many a horse you see careering around a jumping course.

A word of warning if you are jumping your horse and he is the kind of horse that has difficulty working on the bit. A horse, while he is jumping, needs to stretch the whole of his frame to the maximum. The task of jumping is physically strenuous and he uses most of his body to launch himself over a jump. The horse knows that he needs to use all of his body to jump and may think he is incapable of jumping at the same time as being on the bit. If his back is not supple you will already be stretching it by asking him to be on the bit. If you ask a horse such as this to jump while on the bit he will not be able to cope with the double effort that is required by both being on the bit and jumping. You will almost certainly panic and frighten your horse if this is the case. Better wait until the horse is happily going on the bit before you ask him to jump while on it.

There is another aspect to jumping a horse in the round and low outline that a young or novice horse will often adopt while on the bit and that is one of vision. If the horse's head is low and the jump is of any height he will be unable to see to the top of the jump. It is therefore vital to allow the horse to hold his head where he is comfortable and able to view everything well in the approach to the jump. If one thinks of the last four strides as the time in which the horse sorts himself out then the rider should interfere as little as possible with him at this time. During this time he needs to be able to assess as well as he can the height and shape of what he is about to jump. Any checking that takes place should be before those last four strides.

4

Bits etc. and How They Work

The bit is the most important link between a rider and his horse. It is a vital communication tool.

There are many bits to choose from which all have a different action. If you are to choose the correct bit for your horse you must understand how each bit works. You must also know the shape of the horse's mouth to understand how the bit will work in it. Even more importantly you must know the shape of your own horse's mouth – they are not all the same – which is why some horses will go well in one bit and not another. Do not necessarily accept that what the horse has always gone in is the best bit for him. Be intelligent and look at the inside shape of the mouth – how big his tongue is, how wide his mouth is, how high the roof of his mouth is and most importantly at the width and shape of his bars. Many people experiment with different bits to find out which bit is the correct bit for their horse. People rarely use their intelligence and work out how each bit works and how it will suit the shape of their horse's mouth or their horse's particular problem – if he has one. Presumably this is because they don't understand how each bit works.

The temperament of your horse is also important in choosing the correct bit. If he is a strong willed horse that evades you or runs away from you, a stronger bit will obviously be needed until he learns to respect your control. Enthusiastic horses in excitable situations, such as hunting, may never be able to control their emotions enough to listen to your commands and may always need a strong bit.

The width of the bit
The bit should be the correct width for the horse's mouth. The rings of the bit should sit happily at either side of the mouth. The corners of the mouth should not be too close to the rings, or the joints, as this may cause rubbing and pinching, particularly if you are using a loose ringed bit. If the bit is too wide and appears outside the mouth of the horse the bit will slide from side to side in the horse's mouth – it will be uncomfortable and also it will not be giving clear instructions to the horse as it slides around.

To find the width of the bit, measure the actual bit itself (the part that goes in the mouth) from ring to ring or joint to joint; do not measure the joint.

The fitting of the bit
It is sometimes difficult to know exactly where in the mouth of the horse the bit should lie. We are told that the bit, when in the horse's mouth, should just crease the corners of the mouth, but how much should it crease them? Too much of a crease and the bit would be uncomfortable for the horse, pulling on and stretching its mouth more than necessary. Too little of a crease and the bit hangs limply and rather ineffectively in the mouth – it may even start to hit the lower teeth.

To check if your bit is correctly sited stand in front of the horse's head. Take hold of both side pieces of the bridle just above the bit and gently pull down on them so that you remove any slack. When you have done this, the creases in the corners of the mouth should no longer be there. The bit should just be touching the lower edges of the corners of the mouth. If this is the case the bit on your bridle is fitted correctly. If there is a gap between the corners and the bit, it is too low in the mouth. The side pieces need to be shortened. If, on the other hand, the mouth still creases after you have made the side pieces taut, they are too short and need to be lengthened.

The thickness of the bit

The finer the bit the harsher the bit. Think of the thinness of cheese wire and how easily it cuts through cheese. Because it is thin it pushes hard on a small area. If the wire were thicker there would not be enough pressure per square inch to force it through the cheese. In the same way, a fat bit spreads the same amount of pressure over a greater area and therefore exerts less pressure over each square inch. The more pressure per square inch the greater likelihood there is of inflicting pain on the horse and vice versa. Try an experiment on yourself with thin and thick rope or wire. Wrap each one in turn around your wrist and pull hard. You will notice how much more you feel the thinner variety. Fig. 39 makes it obvious.

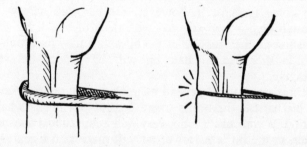

Fig. 39 Wrap each one in turn around your wrist and pull – see which one hurts the most.

A fat bit, that is one whose surface area is greater, like a rubber bit, spreads the pressure and therefore shouldn't inflict any pain or indeed much pressure in the horse's mouth. If the horse has sensitive bars or tongue this thickness of bit may be needed but if the bars are insensitive or average you may find that using a bit like this means the horse barely notices its presence and doesn't respect it. Another disadvantage of a thick bit is the amount of room it takes up in the horse's mouth.

You may find there is not enough room for it to sit comfortably. This will depend on the size of the horse's mouth. If a fat bit is used on a horse with a small mouth it means the horse cannot shut its mouth properly. It probably isn't comfortable with this thickness of bit and it certainly doesn't look very smart. A narrower bit sits more comfortably in the mouth. The horse is able to close his mouth and looks less ridiculous. It is a matter of priority. If the horse has a very sensitive mouth you may not have any choice.

Sensitive/insensitive mouth

Be aware of the width of the bars in your horse's mouth – if they are wide or well covered with flesh or if there is a fat, insensitive, large tongue overlapping the bars they will lack sensitivity to the pressure of the bit. You will need a narrower bit to increase the pressure so that the horse feels it. If, however, the bars are narrow or pointed or not well covered with flesh they will be very sensitive to the pressure of the bit and it may hurt him. If this is the case a fatter bit will be gentler but still effective.

Ultimately it will depend on your control requirements, as the harsher the bit the more control you hope to have with it. If your horse is not very well behaved and does not listen to the bit, a narrower bit will make him listen to it better. But there can be other reasons why a horse doesn't listen to the bit and hence other solutions.

Potential places of pressure
The poll

Pressure on the poll pushes the head lower.

Running reins, Chambons and de Gogues use poll pressure.

The bars

Pressure on the bars brings the horse's head away from that pressure.

All bits except bitless bridles should put pressure on the bars.

The corners of the mouth

Fig. 40 Pressure on the corners of the mouth.

The only bit that intentionally uses pressure on the corners of the mouth is the gag snaffle. It is used to ask the horse to lift his head.

There is a degree of pressure on the lips with the snaffle bit depending on the angle of the horse's head.

Draw reins also lift the horse's head by putting pressure on the corners of the mouth.

The nose

Pressure on the nose pushes the horse's head away from that pressure towards his chest.

The nose is very sensitive and therefore bits or nosebands that exert pressure here can be severe and can inflict pain on the horse.

The Hackamore (or bit-less bridle) puts pressure on the nose. The Kineton noseband also puts pressure on the nose when a contact is taken up with the reins. The drop, flash or grakle nosebands only put pressure on the nose when the horse tries to open his mouth and evade the action of the bit.

The tongue

Pressure on this would bring the head back towards the rider. The tongue differs in its sensitivity from horse to horse. A horse with a thin tongue would obviously be more sensitive than a horse with a fat tongue. The amount of pressure felt by the tongue can be increased by the use of bits such as the Dr. Bristol (the edge of a square plate pushes against the tongue) or the sharp edges of the twisted snaffle.

When a jointed snaffle is used, if the horse's tongue is not overlarge it should fit in the gap between the bars and the V shape that the bit makes when a contact is taken up. In this case there should be very little pressure on the tongue. If the horse's tongue is large and lies over the bars when the bit presses on the tongue, it squashes it and spreads it across the bars, stopping contact of the bit with the bars. There will be a lot of pressure on the tongue and not much, if any, on the bars. A straight bar of any type will place more pressure on the tongue than a jointed or mullen mouth snaffle or a bit with a port which all allow room for the tongue.

Some people wrap chamois leather around the bit. Because the horse dislikes the taste/feel of it he does not like his tongue near it. He, therefore, respects the presence of the wrapped bit on his tongue and relaxes his jaw to get away from it.

The curb (or chin) groove

Because the bones at this point are fairly sharp and not covered with much flesh, this is a fairly sensitive area. The curb chain or strap lies in this groove but its purpose is not to apply pressure. Its purpose is to hold the bit in place as it applies pressure to the bars. Some pressure on the chin groove is inevitable as the curb chain and bit tighten around the horse's lower jaw. It is undesirable that this

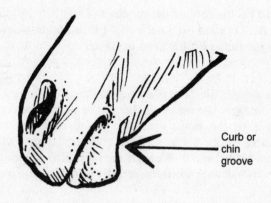

Curb or
chin
groove

Fig. 41 Position of the curb or chin groove.

pressure should hurt the horse because it would mean that
the horse would lift his head up away from the source of
pain. As we want our horse to relax his jaw and keep his
head down, the fitting of the curb chain should be as
comfortable as possible and should always be twisted so
that the links of the chain lie smoothly against the jaw of
the horse. Often the curb chain will be covered with a
softer material such as rubber or leather to be sure that the
chain doesn't hurt.

The roof of the mouth

The roof of the mouth must be one of the most sensitive
areas. It would never normally be desirable to put pressure
on it. The only bit which deliberately does this (one hopes)
is called a Chiffney.

The other occasion when pressure may be put on the
roof of the mouth would be (hopefully unintentionally)
when a bit with a large port, designed to make room for an
over large tongue, pivots upwards and hits the palate. This
is more likely to occur when the horse has a low palate. In
this situation a smaller port or a mullen mouthed bit must
be tried. It could also happen if a jointed snaffle bit was too
large. When the sides of the bit come together the joint lifts

and could hit the roof of the mouth.

The effect of pressure on the roof of the mouth would be to make the horse lift his head in the air.

Copper
With the copper bit there is more relaxation of the jaw and a softer contact. The reason is thought to be that the copper is warmer in the horse's mouth, which makes it more comfortable for the horse. Because they are happier with it they relax better onto it. Wearing the bit is also supposed to cause the horse to produce more saliva, making the mouth moist.

I honestly can't say that the copper feels any warmer to me but, having put it in my mouth, I have noticed a different taste from that of stainless steel. I suspect the reason why horses don't lean on these bits is because they are not too pleasant for the horse to taste and therefore they are not very disposed to put their tongues around it. Perhaps the reason the horse relaxes his jaw could be so that he can get away from the taste. The relaxation of the jaw on its own would be sufficient to produce saliva.

If taste is the reason for the success of this bit, then the fatter the bit the more effective the bit would be, because there is more of the bit to taste. This, of course, is the opposite of the way in which the thickness of the bit normally works. I use a very fat, very round French link which if ordinary rules had applied would have been totally ignored by my horse yet she comes onto the bit and relaxes beautifully.

Copper is a metal that can become brittle in a similar manner to nickel and should therefore be watched for signs of deterioration.

THE ACTION OF THE BIT
The bit is a mechanical tool. Different bits have different mechanical actions. They work in different ways, pivot differently and apply pressure in different places. The following are diagrams and descriptions of several bits, nosebands and martingales showing how they work and where they apply pressure. There are many more bits on

the market than are shown below: the others work on the same principles.

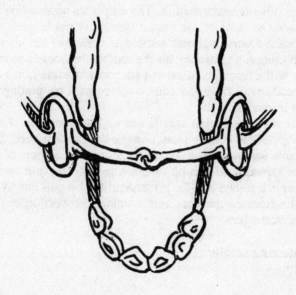

Fig. 42 Jointed eggbut snaffle in position.

Jointed eggbut snaffle

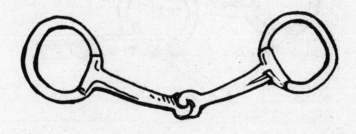

Fig. 43 Jointed eggbut snaffle.

The snaffle bit has a nutcracker action. Before a contact is taken up with the reins the snaffle bit would lie fairly flat across the horse's tongue. When a contact is taken up it brings the rings and the sides of the bit closer together and the joint of the bit rises in the horse's mouth allowing room for the tongue underneath it. The bit places pressure on the top and the sides of the bars. If the bit is too large or the roof of the horse's mouth too close to the bit, the joint of the bit when it rises may hit the roof of the horse's mouth. This will cause considerable pain and make the horse lift its head away from the source of the pain by putting its head in the air.

Because the eggbut snaffle has no loose rings in which the skin of the horse's mouth can be caught or rubbed, it is possible for the rings to lie quite close to the corners of the horse's mouth. If the bit is not too large the nutcracker action is lessened and the pressure of the bit will mostly be on the front of the bars and a smaller proportion on the sides of the bars.

Loose ring snaffle

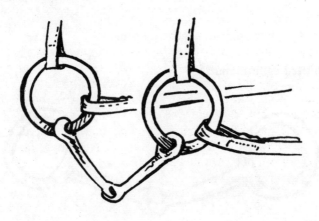

Fig. 44 Loose ring snaffle.

This bit works in the same way as the eggbut snaffle but it is more mobile and versatile in the hands of its rider compared to the eggbut. The loose rings allow the bit to sit more softly in the horse's mouth. Because the bit is able to, and does, slide around the rings of the bit it is possible for the skin of the horse's mouth to be pinched in them. It is, therefore, essential that the rings are placed away from the corners of the mouth. To accomplish this it is normally necessary to use a slightly larger bit so that the ends of the bit lie outside the horse's mouth. Failing this, one can put rubber guards, sometimes called biscuits, between the mouth and the rings to stop this chaffing.

Straight bar snaffle

Fig. 45 Straight bar snaffle.

Because the straight bar snaffle has no joint or port or arch, as in the mullen mouth bit (page 102), there is no room for the tongue under the bit. Pressure will be largely on the tongue. This can be uncomfortable for the horse and may encourage him to put his tongue over the bit. The straight bar snaffle applies pressure in one direction only and that is directly downward on the bars/tongue. It is often thought of as a gentler bit than the jointed snaffle but because it has a tendency to squash the tongue it can be more severe.

Fulmer snaffle
As you can see from fig. 46, the Fulmer snaffle applies pressure to the sides, or cheeks, of the horse's face, pushing and pulling the horse's head in the direction you wish him to go. It is easier for you to make the horse go in a certain direction and easier for the horse to understand that you want him to turn. The cheek-pieces on the Fulmer

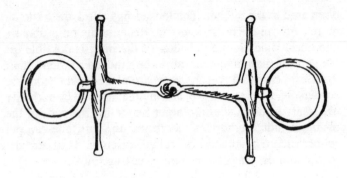

Fig. 46 Fulmer snaffle.

should have loops, attaching them to the cheek pieces on the bridle, which keep the bit steady and fixed in the horse's mouth. It is quite an inflexible bit. It suits those horses that have a tendency to mess with their bits too much, but doesn't give the rider a sensitive feedback from the horse or a sensitive communicating tool.

Mullen mouth bit

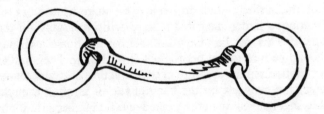

Fig. 47 Mullen mouth bit.

The mullen mouth bit is similar to a straight bar bit but, instead of being straight, the bit is scooped out, thus allowing a gap for the tongue. The bit doesn't squash the tongue and allows the bit to place pressure on the bars.

Bits with ports

A port is only used on bits with a lever action such as a Pelham (page 111) and a Weymouth (page 107). Before the lever is operated, the port lies flat along the tongue, pointing upwards towards the throat of the horse. When the lever operates, the bit twists in the horse's mouth and the port lifts up towards the palate, as shown in fig. 48. The theory is that as it lifts, it allows room for the tongue underneath. The size of the port should depend on the size of the tongue. If, as explained earlier, the port is very high and the roof of the mouth not so high it is possible for the port to hit the roof of the mouth. The height of the horse's palate as well as the size of the horse's tongue should be taken into consideration when choosing a port for your horse's mouth. A horse who has a tendency to put his tongue over the bit would find this more difficult in a bit with a port. The bigger the port the harder he would find it.

Chiffney

The Chiffney is a bit that is used to lead horses that pull back or rear when led. The front part of the bit is placed in the horse's mouth. When the lead rope at the back is pulled downwards, the front of the bit lifts and hits the roof of the horse's mouth. Imagine someone on the ground leading the horse with the lead rope. If the horse pulls backwards the rope will automatically be pulled down. The theory is that knowing that pulling back or rearing will cause him pain the horse will stop pulling back or rearing and avoid putting pressure on the lead rope. This bit is sometimes used on horses who are difficult to load in a trailer or horse box. As the horse pulls back against the person who is leading it the rope will become taut and the bit will literally swing into action. Because of its severe action the person leading the horse needs to be careful using it. The horse should not be dragged along with this bit – this would inflict quite a lot of pain on him and the horse would not learn the lesson of the bit i.e. walk forward = no pain, stop walking or pull back = pain. He should be encouraged to walk alongside the person leading him. It is only if the horse rears or backs up that the action of the bit should

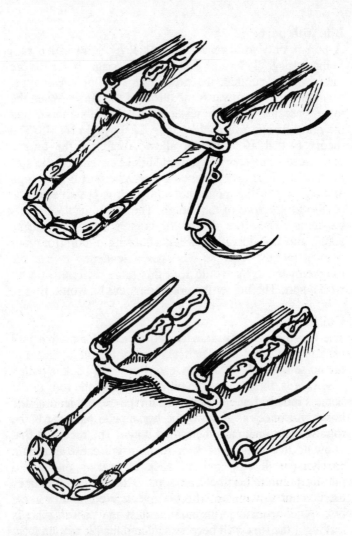

Fig. 48 Ports. When the lever operates, the port lifts up, as shown in the lower picture.

come in. The horse must be made to realise that it is his disobedience that causes the hurt, not the person leading him. It is a severe bit to use, causing pain to the horse in its action and should preferably only be brought out when all

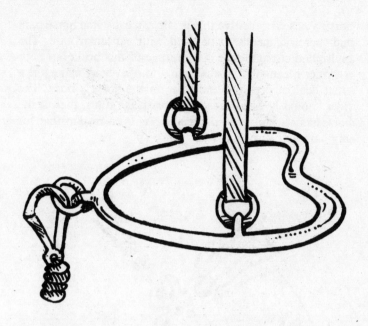

Fig. 49 Chiffney.

else has failed. Remember that fear may be the reason the horse pulls back and that injudicious use of this bit would make the fear much worse.

Hackamore

The Hackamore bridle has no bit. All the controls for steering and slowing or stopping are centred in the nose-band. The noseband has two long metal cheek-pieces hanging down on either side of it. The reins are attached to the ends of these cheek-pieces. Though there is no pressure on the bars of the horse's mouth it has a severe action on the nose of the horse. When a contact is taken up with the reins the cheek-pieces swing backwards and upwards causing the nose band and the back strap to tighten around the whole of the horse's jaw not just the lower jaw. This puts a great deal of pressure on the nose of the horse bringing the head of the horse down towards the horse's chest. As the horse's nose is sensitive this bridle can cause the horse pain and therefore needs to be used with particular care. The multiplied strength that the leverage of this bridle gives to the rider means that a small amount of contact can exert a great deal of pressure and pain on the horse's nose. The rider should have a soft contact with the reins, then if the horse resists and lifts his head he will be responsible for any pain he causes himself.

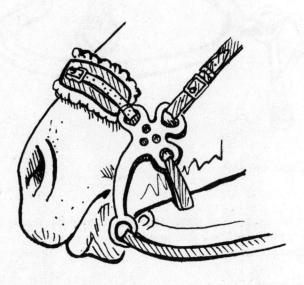

Fig. 50 Hackamore.

Double bridle
The double bridle consists of two bits – a Bridoon and a Weymouth.

Bridoon
The Bridoon is a snaffle bit and has its own set of reins. It should lie just above the Weymouth bit in the horse's mouth. It hangs from the main head piece of the bridle on top of the headpiece holding the Weymouth bit.

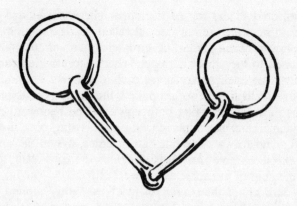

Fig. 51 Bridoon.

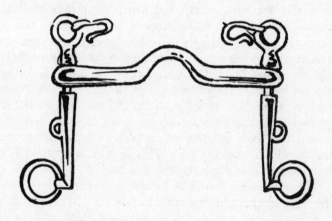

Fig. 52 Weymouth bit.

Weymouth bit

The Weymouth bit has a totally different action from the snaffle bit. It works on the principle of a lever movement that substantially increases the strength of the rider's hands making this a potentially severe bit. The Weymouth bit has cheek-pieces both above and below the bit. The headpiece is attached to the top of the upper cheek-pieces and the reins (the curb reins) are attached to the bottom of the lower cheek-pieces. A curb chain, or strap, is also attached to the top of the upper cheek-piece which comes around the back of the horse's chin and lies in the curb groove. When the reins are pulled, the bottom cheek-piece turns in an arc pivoting both upwards and backwards. At the same time the upper cheek-pieces swing both downwards and forwards by the same degree. When the upper cheek-pieces pivot forwards this pulls the curb chain tight on the chin of the horse as shown in fig. 53 A. The bit and the curb chain then wrap themselves tightly around the lower jaw of the horse. Because of the power of the lever action, the slightest of contacts from the rider's hands can cause considerable pain to the horse. To avoid this pain the horse submits to the rider's will. It is essential that the rider uses this bit both gently and sensitively, releasing the contact instantly the horse submits. How essential this is cannot be stressed enough. If the bit causes him discomfort and he tries to reduce this discomfort by doing as you ask, the discomfort must stop immediately. He has to know he has got it right. In other words nose in the air = pain. Nose vertical = no pain. If the pressure and the pain remained when he relaxed onto the bit he would be confused. He would have learnt nothing except perhaps that coming onto the bit didn't stop the pain. This is why it is so VERY important to ride correctly with this bit.

The curb chain should be turned round carefully so that the rings of chain lie smoothly against the jaw (for greater comfort still use a rubber or leather curb guard). It is most important that this chain does not cause pain to the chin, as this would encourage the horse to lift its head away from this pain. This is opposite to the effect that we wish the bit to have.

Because it is very important to hold the reins of the Weymouth bit so carefully and ride so accurately with them, it is essential that, before using a double bridle, a rider must have a totally independent and secure seat, and have developed careful, responsive hands. The rider must be capable of remaining in balance in the saddle without

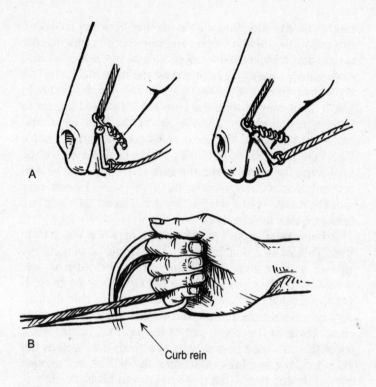

Curb rein

Fig. 53
A The curb chain on the left is loose. The picture on the right shows how, when contact is taken with the curb rein, the lower cheek-piece comes back and the upper cheek-piece swivels forwards, pulling the curb rein tight.
B How to hold two sets of reins.

ever needing the support of the reins to remain in position.

When using the double bridle the rider will have two sets of reins to contend with. This takes a little time to get used to – even for a proficient rider – and it is worth taking some time practising holding and using two sets of reins before you get on the horse. There is more than one correct way to hold two sets of reins. I find the following method the best. The Weymouth or curb rein is held under the little finger, the rein then passing between the thumb and first finger. The snaffle or bridoon rein is held between the little finger and the ring finger then passing between the index finger and the middle finger. Holding them in this manner means that they are held independently of each other and each rein can easily be adjusted by the other hand (fig. 53 B). When the horse is working on the bit there should hardly be a contact with the curb rein; it should appear to hang almost loosely. The weight of the rein is usually sufficient to remind the horse of its presence. If the horse fights the presence of the bit by lifting his head he will be increasing the contact with the curb rein and hence he will be responsible for tightening the curb chain. Horses very quickly realise when their action has caused pain and are usually quick to remedy it.

A horse usually isn't as forward going when you start to use a Pelham or a double bridle. This would be particularly true of a horse that finds being on the bit difficult and would normally resist accepting the bit. When the horse is put in a double bridle or Pelham you are more able to insist that he comes onto the bit and relaxes his jaw. When he does this he is stretching part of the top line, i.e. the neck, more than it would normally be stretched. If as well as this he is working in a forward manner this will stretch another part of the top line – that is the hocks and his back. He will probably find stretching both ends of the top line quite difficult and therefore will resist the extra effort required of him. He will often hang back behind the leg and not really go forwards. At first he will deserve a certain amount of latitude but gradually you need to insist that the work is as forward going as it was before. Most people would say that a horse shouldn't be ridden in a double bridle (or a Pelham, see page 111) until he is working in a forward going manner and is obedient to the leg. There is a lot of truth in this. If you are unable to get the horse to work energetically in a snaffle bit there is no way that you could get him to work with any degree of impulsion in a Pelham or a double bridle.

The lever action of the Weymouth bit is supposed to put pressure on the poll of the horse thus pushing his head down. As you can see from the description above, this bit is designed to work by tightening the curb chain and bit around the horse's lower jaw. It is not designed to create poll pressure. Perhaps the reason people assumed that it asserted pressure on the poll was because as the upper cheek pieces pivoted forwards it pulled the side pieces down. As a result there was potential pressure on both the poll and the corners of the mouth. The poll is a fixed object whereas the corners of the mouth are stretchy. Therefore instead of putting pressure on the poll and making the horse lower its head the bit will lift in the horse's mouth creasing its corners more than usual.

However, there is a circumstance in which poll pressure may be created. This is when the horse is above the bit. If his head were above the vertical and he was fighting the action of the bit by pushing against it with his teeth, the hold that the horse has on the bit provides a fulcrum for the bit to pivot on. When the upper cheek pieces pivot forwards and down, it tightens the leather between the poll and the mouth. Because the bit is fixed against the teeth it cannot ride up in the horse's mouth and therefore pressure will be placed on the poll and the horse should be persuaded to lower his head. As above, the tightening of the curb chain will restrict the amount of pressure that can be put on the poll.

Pelham
This bit, which is illustrated in fig. 54, is a combination of the two bits of the double bridle, that is the Weymouth and the Bridoon, and broadly speaking has the same effect. There are two sets of reins: the upper set, attached to the upper or snaffle rings, and the other set attached to the curb rings, which are at the bottom of the cheek pieces. It should be used with two reins, though can be used with a D rein or joining reins (see page 113). When a contact is taken up with the rein attached to the snaffle rings, the bit works as a snaffle. When contact is taken up with the reins attached to the bottom of the curb cheeks, the bit acts as a Weymouth bit. It is intended to be the same or similar to a combination of both of the bits of the double bridle, but without having two bits in the horse's mouth. Again it is most important that when the horse is working in a correct position there is

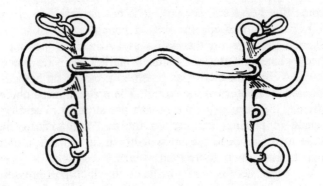

Fig. 54 Pelham.

absolutely no pressure on the curb rein – the contact should be almost non-existent. Everything that has been written above about the Weymouth bit applies to using the curb rein on the Pelham.

The curb chain is often put through the upper rings of the Pelham bit. This has the advantage of keeping the curb chain in place but the disadvantage of pressing the rings tightly against the face of the horse whenever the action of the bit is used.

Hanging cheek snaffle

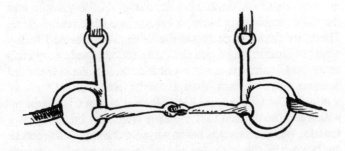

Fig. 55 Hanging cheek snaffle.

This bit is very similar to the ordinary snaffle but has two cheeks which extend upwards from the snaffle rings. On top of these cheeks are two smaller rings. Instead of the bridle's cheek-pieces being attached to the snaffle rings, as the reins are, they are attached to these smaller rings.

The action of the hanging cheek snaffle is very similar to that of the ordinary snaffle but there are some differences. Rather like the loose ring snaffle it is a flexible bit. Some argue that because of the height of the cheek pieces this snaffle has a lever action. Their theory is that when the contact is increased it puts a backwards pressure on the snaffle rings causing the upper cheek-pieces to rotate forwards and down. Just as with the Weymouth bit without a curb chain, the bit will merely lift in the horse's mouth unless the horse holds the bit between his teeth. However, because there are no lower cheek-pieces, any pivoting of the bit is very, very minimal and hence all the possible effects described above are also very, very minimal.

There is less play in this snaffle compared to the loose ring snaffle and this does give this bit a slightly more accurate feel.

D rein

Sometimes, particularly when children ride in a Pelham and find it difficult to cope with two reins, a leather D rein is used between the two bits and a single rein is attached to this D rein. This creates an action somewhere between the action of the two reins. It has a slight lever action and if the curb chain is adjusted correctly this will be enough to increase its pressure on the curb groove, and hence of the bit on the bars, without ever allowing it to become very tight or painful. Its disadvantage is that this pressure tends to be fairly constant because a contact has to be maintained with both bits at all times.

Joining rein

It is also possible to use a joining rein to go between the two rings of a Pelham instead of a D rein. These are two straight reins that join and attach to the main rein. Using this it is possible to make the main rein effective on either the snaffle bit or the curb bit. Which rein is the most effective will depend on the height of the rider's hands – if

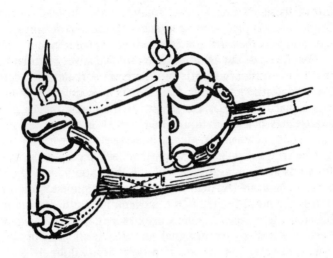

Fig. 56 D rein.

they are held higher than normal the curb rein will be effective. If the hands are held low the snaffle rein will be the functioning bit. If the hands are held somewhere in the middle the effect will be diffused between the two reins.

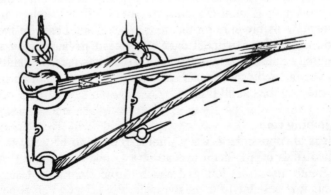

Fig. 57 Joining rein.

Kimblewick

This bit is a Pelham with very short cheek pieces. It is used with only one rein and this is attached to large rings beside the bit. Because the reins slide to the top of the metal rings its action is predominantly that of a snaffle. If the rider puts his or her hands down the horse's shoulders it alters the position of the rein in the rings and can make the action more like that of a curb rein.

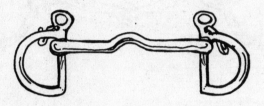

Fig. 58 Kimblewick.

Gag

The gag rein is attached to a smooth piece of rope that slides through holes made in the rings of the bit. The rope is then attached to the headpiece that goes over the poll of the horse. The intention is that, when any pressure is taken up on the gag rein, the smooth rope will pull through the rings of the bit and shorten the distance of rope and leather between the poll and the lips of the horse. Because the lips of the horse are soft and stretchy they are the areas of least resistance compared to the density of the poll and the bit will therefore pull up on the lips. The horse will then lift his head to stop the sensation. Horses that have a tendency to throw their heads down and tank off with their riders will be better behaved with this bit.

The gag rein is normally used with another rein attached directly to the ring. This other rein should be used most of the time. The gag rein should only be used as a corrective aid if the horse refuses to submit to his rider's control and puts his head down. When the horse has obeyed the rider and lifted his head the rider should revert to the other rein. This other rein has the action of an ordinary snaffle rein.

Fig. 59 Gag.

Continental snaffle, Dutch gag or bubble bit
The rider has the choice of attaching the reins to any of the rings from the large ring to the two smaller rings beneath. If the reins are attached to the lower rings the bit will have a stronger action. The cheek pieces attach to the small upper rings.

Fig. 60 Continental snaffle.

If the horse has a habit of putting his head down too low and running away with his rider, the bit will perform like a normal gag, pulling up on the corners of the mouth and encouraging the horse to lift his head. Like the Weymouth and Pelham, when the lower cheek-pieces are pulled back by the reins, the upper cheek-piece swivels forwards and down. Unlike the Weymouth and Pelham this bit has no curb chain and therefore nothing to stop the upper cheek-pieces swivelling forwards to their full extent. This shortens the distance between the bit and the poll, potentially putting pressure on both the poll and the corners of the mouth. The corners of the mouth are stretchy and offer the least resistance and the bit will therefore pull on them rather than exert pressure on the poll. Just as with the ordinary gag this will have the effect of lifting the horse's head.

Cavesson noseband

This is a standard noseband. It should be possible to fit two fingers placed sideways between it and the nose of the horse. It is only intended to put any pressure on the nose if the horse opens its mouth in an attempt to avoid the control of the bit. In other words the horse will be the one putting the pressure on his nose. This noseband can be used with all bits and must be used with the double bridle, Pelham and Kimblewick.

Kineton noseband

The Kineton noseband is hooked around the snaffle bit. As the reins are pulled back the noseband also comes backwards and tightens around the horse's nose. The horse should bring its head away from the pressure of the noseband, accepting the action of the bit. Because the noseband is attached to the bit it tends to keep the bit forwards in the horse's mouth, putting less pressure on the bars as the nose takes the pressure of the reins.

Drop noseband

This noseband is specifically designed for the many horses that try to avoid the control of the bit by opening their

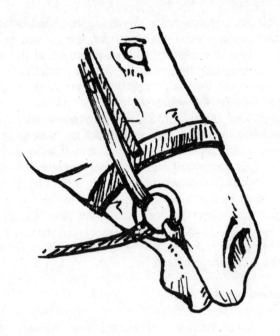

Fig. 61 Cavesson noseband.

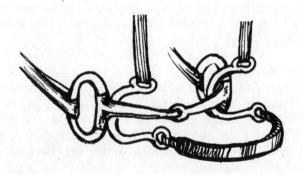

Fig. 62 Kineton noseband.

mouths. When they open their mouths they are pulling their bottom jaws back away from a contact with the bit.

This means that the bit no longer lies on the bars of the mouth and the rider no longer has any contact with, or control of, his or her horse. A drop noseband doesn't fit above the bit, like the cavesson. It is angled so that it comes underneath the bit and fastens in the chin groove. It is quite a difficult noseband to fit correctly. To be effective it needs to be fairly tight and there should be only one finger rather than two between the noseband and the nose. It is essential that it does not lie on the soft part of the nose, i.e. the part that lies between the nostrils because this is extremely sensitive. This noseband should only be used in conjunction with a snaffle bridle. These nosebands and the ones that follow are also used to stop horses that have developed a habit of putting their tongues over the bit. The horse's inability to open his mouth stops him from lifting his tongue over the bit.

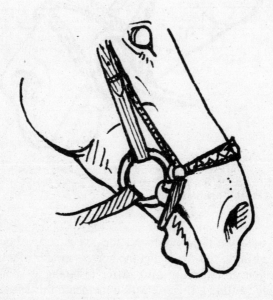

Fig. 63 Drop noseband.

Flash noseband

To the front of an ordinary cavesson noseband a strap is attached at an angle taking it down underneath the bit. It is much easier to fit correctly than a drop noseband though it serves exactly the same purpose. The lower strap can either be stitched onto the cavesson as above or added by means of a converter strap. They both work in the same way. Again this noseband should only be used with a snaffle bridle.

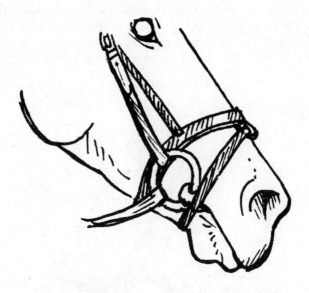

Fig. 64 Flash noseband.

As with the drop noseband the lower strap should be fastened fairly tightly so that the horse's mouth is held shut when you are working him. After fastening it should be possible to slide a finger easily underneath this strap.

It is still essential that there is no pressure from the front of the noseband on the soft part of the nose, so ensure that the noseband is not too low on the face of the horse. The lower strap should be fitted neatly just underneath the bit and care should be taken that the buckle should not be fastened near the lips of the horse as this can cause pressure and soreness.

Grakle noseband

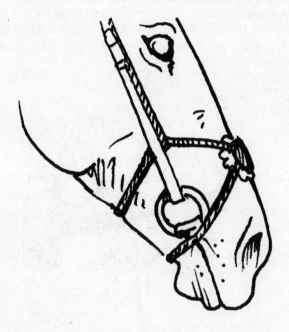

Fig. 65 Grakle noseband.

The Grakle noseband is similar to the flash noseband but, rather than being attached to a wide leather cavesson, the upper part of the noseband is also narrow and angled upwards slightly. Because of this increased angle the power of the noseband spreads over a greater area. Because the strap is thinner it puts much pressure on the nose and jaw of the horse if he tries to open his mouth or cross his jaw. There is a strap at the back of a Grakle that joins both nosebands and stops the upper band from riding too high on the jaw of the horse.

Running martingales

The running martingale links the underside of the girth with the reins. It is made of a wide strap of leather, which buckles around the girth on one end. At the other end the rein splits in two and attaches to each rein by means of two metal rings. The reins are able to slide through these rings but rubber stops should always be put on the reins about one foot from the bit to stop the martingale rings slipping too close to the bit.

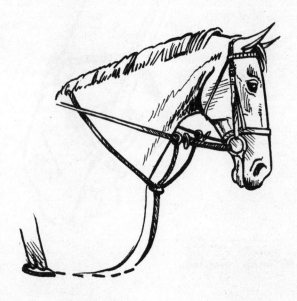

Fig. 66 Running martingale.

When the horse lifts his head the martingale tightens on the reins and stops the horse from lifting his head any higher. It will only stop the horse from putting his head high. It is not able to bring the horse's head onto the bit. It is used on horses that throw their heads in the air. The running martingale alters the angle of the reins when the horse lifts his head so that the rider can maintain some control of his horse and stop him from putting his head any higher. It is a fairly effective device and not too severe as it acts on the reins rather than on the noseband. The straps of the running martingale should be long enough to have no effect on the reins when the horse's head is in the correct position.

Fig. 67 The running martingale working to stop the horse lifting his head.

It is not unusual for a horse on a cross country course to be wearing a running martingale, even if he is not one disposed to lifting his head to high. When riding cross country it helps the horse to move and jump freely if he is allowed to lift and stretch his neck. Sometimes a horse can become difficult to stop or check when he is galloping freely like this and the use of a running martingale can give the rider an extra strength of brake by using it as a lever when required.

Standing martingales
The standing martingale is also designed to stop the horse from throwing his head in the air. It also has a leather strap which buckles around the girth but it does not divide in two and the other end of this martingale buckles itself at the back of a cavesson noseband. If the horse does attempt to lift his head he will feel pressure on the front of his nose which will be very unpleasant for him. The length of the martingale must be sufficient to allow the horse to hold his head in a comfortable position and it should not be used to pull the horse onto the bit.

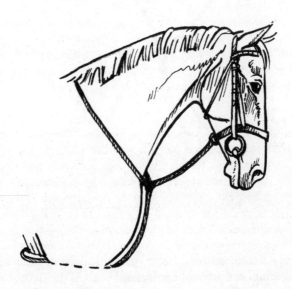

Fig. 68 Standing martingale.

The standing martingale should never be used for jumping as it restricts the amount the horse can stretch his neck. When he jumps he needs to stretch the whole of his frame. If it were to be used when jumping, the horse would either hurt himself as he stretched his neck, or he would restrict his body so that he didn't hurt his nose. If he didn't stretch himself he would be very unathletic over the jump. It would be very easy to destroy a horse's confidence over jumps if he were jumped in a standing martingale.

This martingale can be used with the upper cavesson part of a flash noseband but obviously not with a drop or Grakle noseband.

Draw reins

A draw rein is a single rein that goes from the hands of the rider through the ring of the bit on one side, over the horse's head, through the ring of the bit on the other side and back to the hands of the rider.

When the rider takes up a contact with the rein it shortens the distance of the rein between the poll and the bit. This puts pressure on the corner of the lips of the horse. The horse will then lift his head away from this pressure.

Draw reins are always used with ordinary reins and should only be used to ask the horse to lift his head, not to force him. As soon as he does lift his head the contact with the draw reins should cease.

Running reins

Running reins are longer than draw reins. They go from the rider's hands through the rings of the bit and from there they are attached to the girth either between the horse's legs or underneath the rider's legs. The position that they are placed in will depend on the effect required. If they are placed between the horse's legs the effect will be to pull the horse's head lower. If they are placed at the bottom of the saddle flaps, under the rider's legs, it will pull the horse's lower jaw closer to its chest. Running reins should always be used with ordinary reins.

The usefulness of running reins is dubious. If you use them attached to the girth under the saddle flaps you will

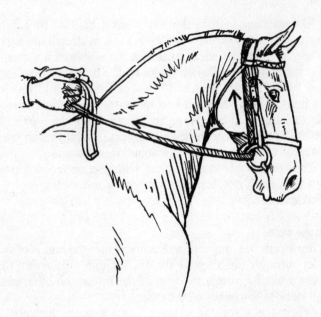

Fig. 69 Draw reins.

be forcing the horse's head onto the bit. It may look good but the force that is pulling the horse back against his will must create tension. What we are seeking to achieve is a horse that relaxes and stretches his neck in order to come onto the bit. When the horse is forced back into this position with running reins there will be no relaxation or stretching of the neck. Instead the neck will be shortened. The restriction made on the neck will mean that the movement of the horse will be restricted throughout his body. When the running reins are removed there will be no improvement in the shape, suppleness or athleticism of the horse.

If the running reins are placed between the forelegs of the horse and attached to the underside of the girth they will have the effect of pulling the horse's head lower.

If you do decide to use running reins try and use them to ask the horse to adopt a different position rather than

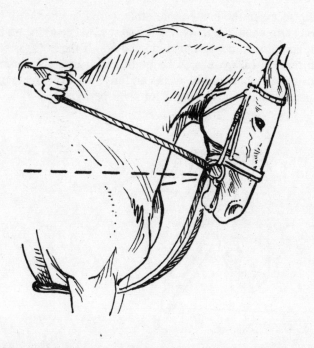

Fig. 70 Running reins. The dotted lines show an alternative position for the running reins.

forcing it there. As soon as he listens to what you ask release the pressure on the running reins.

Chambon

This is designed to be used while the horse is on the lunge and is intended to persuade a horse to work with his back rounded rather than hollowed and to dissuade him from working with his head in a high position. A wide strap is buckled to the underside of the girth. This strap then splits into two and each end is attached to smooth ropes which pass through metal runners lying behind the ears of the horse, and then go down to clips which are attached to the rings of the bit. The Chambon puts pressure on the poll of the horse, encouraging him to work in a long, low outline. This stretches the whole of his spine, or top line, and will help to make the horse more athletic and supple. With his body stretched like this he will find it easier to come on the bit and also to engage his hindquarters. If the horse is stiff on his top line you may be putting him into a strenuous position so it should be used carefully, not over tightening it and initially only using it for short periods.

Fig. 71 Chambon.

De Gogue
This is a similar device to the Chambon but it is designed for use when riding rather than lungeing. Whereas the Chambon is clipped onto the rings of the bit the de Gogue is allowed to run through the rings of the bit and is then clipped onto the ordinary reins. When using the de Gogue the same considerations should be borne in mind as when using the Chambon but if there is any stiffness or discomfort in the horse's back it will be made worse by the weight of the rider.

Fig. 72 De Gogue.

5

Suppling and Strengthening Exercises

Balance of the horse
When we school a horse we have two main aims. Firstly to discipline his mind so that he accepts our domination of him and is obedient to our demands. Secondly we need to exercise his body so that he is physically more able to perform successfully in whatever sphere we are interested in, be it the show ring, cross country or show jumping competitions, the dressage arena and/or the hunting field. For all of these disciplines, after the mental discipline of the horse, the most important aim is that of the improvement of his balance. If he is well balanced he will be more elegant, more powerful and more able to jump.

First, though, we must understand what balance of the horse means.

A human's weight has to be balanced between two legs which, as we have seen, is somewhat precarious. The horse, however, must balance his weight equally over four legs which makes him a much more secure individual. If he has too much weight on the front two of those legs he is unlikely to fall over – unlike ourselves – though obviously he won't be able to perform as well. Like us he can also have too much weight on one side or the other (lateral balance) but again this won't make him feel like he is going to fall over.

A horse would have too much weight on one side of him if his rider were leaning or putting too much weight to one side. He would be unbalanced laterally. If you were carrying a load and that load was slipping to one side you would take a step in the direction in which it was slipping to catch it. You would be stepping under its weight. If a rider leans to one side and unbalances the horse in this direction then the horse will want to take a step that way to catch the rider's weight and correct the imbalance. If the rider had too much weight on his or her right side the horse would automatically want to step to the right (and vice versa).

When a horse is lineally imbalanced it will normally have too much weight on the forehand. This imbalance affects probably 95% of horses and therefore to correct it is the task facing 95% of riders. It helps if we, as humans, can understand how a horse that has too much weight on his forehand feels. If you are interested to know this feeling you can get an idea of it by walking on all fours. Put your fists on the floor and walk with feet and hands as if a four legged animal, something like fig. 73. Our front 'legs' are quite a lot shorter than our 'back' legs and because of this you are placing a vast amount of weight on your hands, very much more 'on the forehand' than any horse. Naturally in this position you are very unathletic. Even though it is an exaggeration it does give you some idea of how a horse feels when he has a lot of weight on his forehand. You couldn't imagine jumping a jump or performing elegantly with your hands pinned down like this.

Remain on all fours. Instead of having your legs straight, gradually bend them and at the same time bring your feet under you, as in fig. 74. Have you noticed that the pressure, or weight, on your hands is reducing and at the same time your 'back' legs are taking more of the weight? Notice in fig. 74 how much your back has been lowered when you bring your legs further underneath you.

Your hands now feel lighter and freer – if you were a horse you would now be more able to jump or look elegant.

Now lower your back and bring your legs even further under your body as in fig. 75 – your hands should feel even lighter.

When you lower your back you put more of the weight of your body onto your legs. In the same way the horse

131

Fig. 73 On all fours.

Fig. 74 Bring your feet under you.

must learn to lower his quarters so that he moves more of his weight onto his back legs. When you put your legs under you and bent your knees (a human equivalent of hocks) this meant that your legs were taking more of the weight of your body, freeing your hands from their burden of weight. In the same way the horse must learn to bend his hocks and put his back legs further under him. By combining all movements – lowering his back, bending his knees

Fig. 75 Bring your legs even further under your body.

and putting his back legs further under him – he reduces further the amount of weight his forehand is supporting and increases that placed on his back legs.

Now you have done this exercise and pretended to be a horse can you imagine how much more athletic a horse must feel if he is able to lighten his forehand like this? You know how cumbersome you felt while walking on all fours. Hopefully it will give you a good indication of the difference we can make to our horse by training him to lower his quarters, bend his hocks and put them further under him. While you were in this position you should also have noticed that it puts strain on your calves and thighs. The horse finds this position hard just as we have done and it takes a lot of training and exercise to make him strong enough to cope with it.

You will probably have heard phrases such as *on the forehand, lowering the quarters, engaging the hindquarters, engaging the hocks*, and *balance of the horse* many times. Hopefully they will make more sense to you now.

The balanced horse

Fig. 76 The balanced horse.

You can see how the horse in fig. 76 is light in the forehand and that his hind legs are coming powerfully under him.

The unbalanced horse

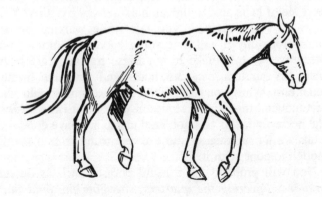

Fig. 77 The unbalanced horse.

The horse in fig. 77 is quite different. His hind legs hardly come under him and you can see how much weight there is on his forehand making it heavy and cumbersome. The spine of this horse needs stretching and rounding so that he will find it easier to put his hocks under him and take some of the weight off his forehand.

The hollow backed horse

Fig. 78 The hollow backed horse.

The horse in fig. 78 is different again. Because he holds his head high, it is tempting to think that he is balanced. But in fact the reason his head is high is that his spine is bent the wrong way – it is hollow or concave. This throws his head in the air and keeps his quarters high. His back legs could never come under him because of the shape of his spine. If you look at the diagrams of the horse's spine in Chapter 3 (page 71), horse A is this horse. You can see how he could never bring his back legs under him until he has altered the shape of his spine and become like horse B. Altering the shape of this horse's spine will not be easy because he will find it physically very difficult. Because this horse holds his head so high, he throws some of his weight backwards onto his hind legs thereby improving his balance to a degree and allowing him to move freely. Some show jumping ponies and a lot of Arabs carry themselves like this. It does help them move well and some are very good jumpers but they can never progress beyond the level they are at. Unfortunately when you start to school them they will appear to go backwards at first because the one advantage they had (their high head carriage) you are taking away from them. Eventually though they will change the shape of the spines and make further progress.

The exercises explained in this chapter help the horse in different ways. Some make the horse more supple along his top line, making it easier for him to come onto the bit and bring his hocks well under him. Some exercises make him more supple along his inside length so that he finds it easier to bend his body to the right and to the left. Most of the exercises will make him stronger in his back legs and most of the exercises will improve more than one aspect at once. If you understand what each one does, and how it affects your horse, you should be in a better position to decide which specific exercises particularly suit him.

When you were pretending to be a horse standing on all fours with your back lowered, your knees bent and your feet well under your body, you were imitating a horse achieving balance. Can you remember how much strain this placed on your legs? When you ask the horse to balance himself by putting his hind legs further underneath him he also finds it hard – it is also a strain on his legs. This means that, as well as using exercises to help the horse's back legs stretch to come further underneath him, you also need to use exercises which will strengthen these legs so that he is better able to carry his own weight.

In Chapter 3, we saw that being on the bit can also put a particular strain on that part of the back that lies behind the saddle. This will be the case with a young unmuscled horse or an older horse with either a weak or a stiff back. For them it is almost painful to bring their back legs under them when they are on the bit. Think how most humans feel when trying to touch their toes. Obviously we must have more patience with these horses but we also need to put them through a series of exercises which will help them develop muscles in this region as well as stretching this area. Initially, working on the bit in itself will have a stretching and strengthening effect, and you shouldn't introduce any harder work until the horse has improved a little and is finding being on the bit easier. When this has happened, gradually introduce large circles then a few simple transitions. Round and down, transitions, circles and shoulder-in are the most useful exercises but don't ask the horse to do them for too long until he has gained strength. Remember that at first the work should not be too forward going, as this will also increase the strain your horse feels, and remember as always that the work should never be too demanding.

THE HORSE'S STIFF SIDE

Human beings tend to be more able with one side of their body than the other. Most of us are right-handed and everything we do with the right hand we do very much better than we do with the left hand. Some of us are left-handed and are therefore better with the left hand than the right. With this favoured hand we write better, draw better and we are stronger. In very much the same way horses also have a more able side. They perform better when they are working on either the right rein or the left rein. We call the side that is less able their stiff side. Basically the hind leg on that side isn't working as well as the other hind leg. You can tell which this stiff rein is by the way in which the horse bends or doesn't bend his body when turning to the right or the left. One side will bend easily – the other will feel like it wants to go in a straight line – this is the stiff side. When working on this stiff rein the horse will lean more on your inside hand. This is partly because the inside leg on this rein isn't working as well, isn't coming under the horse as well and therefore isn't carrying the horse as well. He will be asking you to support him with the inside rein and you will know this by the extra weight you feel in this hand and by the way your arm aches later. A horse will also find it more difficult to strike off on the correct leg in canter when he is working on his stiff side because the inside hind leg has to come even further under him.

We can help to correct this 'stiffness' by working on this rein more than the other, and also by not allowing the horse to lean on your hand by having too strong a contact. If you feel weight there, soften your contact so he has nothing to lean on. Your hold of this side of the bit should be light. If the horse tries to take a strong contact, try vibrating the fingers of your hand on this side or by giving and taking the rein by about $\frac{1}{4}$ to $\frac{1}{2}$ an inch. By working the horse on this rein more you will gradually make the weaker leg become stronger and catch up with its more proficient partner. By removing the support of that rein you are making the horse balance himself and step under his own weight (see The wall in Chapter 2 page 35). Be aware of the improvement when it takes place, because eventually the weaker leg should catch up with the other leg and both legs should then be worked to the same degree as the other.

STRAIGHTNESS OF THE HORSE

A horse can never be taught to balance himself unless he is straight. In order for the horse to be straight his back legs must follow in the tracks made by his front legs. If the hind legs don't follow in the tracks of the front legs it is impossible to drive the hind legs further under the horse and encourage him to take more weight.

Riding in a straight line

When a horse is ridden beside a wall or fence, he may often seek mental support from that wall by keeping both the front and the back of his body an equal distance from the wall. Because the horse's body is wider at the back than at the front, this will mean that the back legs will be making tracks further away from the wall than the tracks made by the front legs. Hence his quarters have come in and his body is not straight, as in fig. 79.

To be straight the spine of the horse should point in the direction in which he is going and should be parallel to any

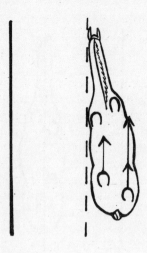

Fig. 79 Not going straight.

wall or boundary he might be working alongside, as in fig. 80.

Because of this the shoulders of the horse are just a little bit further away from the wall than the horse's quarters.

Riding on a circle
When the horse is on a circle his spine should be bent in the same curve as the curve of the circle. His back legs should still follow in the same tracks as his forelegs. In fig. 81 it is the left hand horse whose body is in the correct shape. Sometimes horses, if they are not able to maintain the bend in their body that the circle demands, will allow their hind legs to follow a track that is outside the track of the front two legs. This is termed "falling out of the hindquarters". In fig. 81 the right hand horse is not following the correct bend of the circle with his body – his neck is bent but his body is straight. A stronger aid with the rider's outside leg, placed behind the girth, coupled with the whip should encourage an increased bend in the body and a correct track of the hind legs.

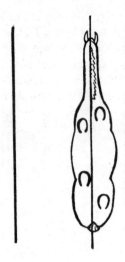

Fig. 80 Going straight.

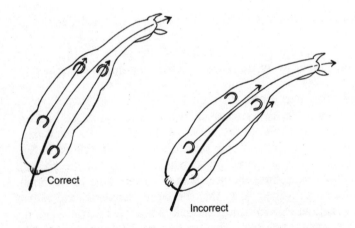

Correct

Incorrect

Fig. 81 On a circle.

Wrong bend

When working on a circle some horses have a tendency to
go round the circle with no bend in their body or with an

140

opposite bend. By doing this they are evading the action of the rein going through their body. This means that, because they are not bending correctly, they are not putting extra weight on the inside hind leg and they do not have to put this leg further underneath them. Basically they are making life easy for themselves. Make sure that the inside rein is bringing the head onto the shape of the circle, the inside leg is pushing the middle of the horse into the bend and the outside leg is pushing the hind quarters into the shape of a circle.

Fig. 82 In wrong bend.

The horse in fig. 82 is in wrong bend – not even his neck is bent to the shape of the circle.

Working in an inside position
When you are working a horse around the arena you are riding two halves of a circle with two long straight bits in between. As the horse goes along the long sides you should

141

ask him for the slightest bend in the direction he is going – as if he were on a very, very large circle – as shown in fig. 83. When he works around the short sides of the arena the bend becomes greater as he is now on a 20 metre circle. So working the arena is the same as working either a very large circle or a 20 metre circle depending where you are on the arena. Therefore you ride the horse just as if you were riding one of those circles, with the aids just the same as for a circle and most particularly working from the inside leg into the outside rein just as described on page 147.

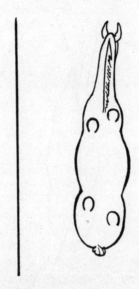

Fig. 83 Horse in an inside position.

The only time in an arena that you would work the horse in a totally straight line is when crossing the arena either on the diagonal or up the centre line.

Why should the horse be straight?
If the horse is not straight his hind legs cannot come properly under his body and the action of the hind legs

would come out at the side of the horse. Also, if the back legs do not take the energy in the direction of the bit the reins are unable to harness the energy of the hind legs. (In lateral work we actually ask the horse's hind legs not to follow in the tracks of the forelegs but it is for a different purpose which will be explained later.)

WORKING ON THE BIT

When the horse is on the bit he is accepting your control, via the bit, by relaxing his jaw and placing his head in such a position that the bit lies on the bars of his mouth. You are able to control him and also control and harness the energy created by the hindquarters. Because he is on the bit his neck is rounded. Because his neck is rounded his back must also be rounded. This means his top line, the line that runs from his nose over the top of his neck along his back and down the back of his legs to his hocks, has to stretch and become more supple. This principle was first described in Chapter 3.

A lot of the exercises that follow develop more energy and strength in the hind leg of the horse. It is essential that the reins are able to capture and harness this energy and power, otherwise it will escape. We are back to the opposing directional forces of the reins and the hind legs. If the horse is not on the bit, the reins cannot capture and use the energy generated by the hind legs and most of the exercises which follow would be of no use. In fact most of the exercises would be impossible to perform unless you have the control that having your horse on the bit gives you.

Working on the bit is both a way of going and an exercise. It must be adopted as the way in which the horse always goes when he is working. It is also an exercise because merely being on the bit helps to supple, stretch and strengthen the horse along the top line. Some horses are naturally very supple along their top line and will find working on the bit quite easy – for them it will hardly be an exercise. Other horses can find it quite difficult to achieve and therefore it is worth taking time with them in this stage of their training and not asking anything too much in the way of exercises whilst they are establishing themselves here. In those early days when the horse has only just begun to accept and work on the bit, it is often enough of an exercise in itself just to work on the bit in the various paces. The horse's natural suppleness/stiffness or weakness/strength along the top line will often dictate how easy or difficult he finds coping with working on the bit. Be aware of how well your horse copes before deciding how long to work in an outline which he may find strenuous. Be sympathetic to the strain that the new outline may cause him if he is not naturally supple or if his back is not naturally in the correct shape.

Working on the bit stretches and therefore supples the whole of the top line of the horse, starting at his poll, running down his neck, back and then down the back legs of the horse to the hocks. When your horse is on the bit he is submitting happily to your control which promotes a happy attitude towards work. The horse must be on the bit in order to harness the power developed by the hindquarters. Hence none of the exercises which follow can be performed properly unless the horse is on the bit.

CIRCLES

Earlier in the book I suggested you ran around in a smallish circle and noticed how much extra weight was being placed on your inside leg. Can I suggest that you do this again to remember the feeling? Make the circles larger and smaller and you will notice that with the larger circles there is less weight being thrown onto your inside leg than when you are running around in a small circle. The smaller the circle the more weight your inside leg carries. In just the same way the horse takes more weight on his inside legs, particularly the hind leg, when he is ridden on a circle. If one leg is taking more weight than the other it follows that the leg which is taking more weight will become stronger than the leg that is not.

Go back to running round in a circle – there is something else to notice. Look down at your feet and see how the inside leg is taking longer strides and coming further forward than the other leg. Watch a horse on a circle and you will see the same thing happening. The inside hind leg takes a longer step than the outside hind leg. This happens naturally and involuntarily. If the horse is on the bit and bent around your inside leg when you work on a circle you will automatically be making his inside hind become stronger and take deeper steps underneath him. As the inside hind leg stretches underneath the horse it also makes the back of the horse stretch (because it is part of the stretchy top line). Obviously this will both supple and strengthen the back of your horse as well as his hind leg. You are on your way to improving his balance because you are stretching the hind leg as it reaches under the horse and strengthening it as it takes more weight. By working on both reins on a circle you can improve the way both hind legs work.

You can see in fig. 84 how the inside hind leg comes right under the body of the horse.

Remember how the weight on your inside leg increased as the circle became smaller. The same happens with horses and though this means that there is more to be gained athletically by working on a smaller circle it also means that the chance of strain becomes greater particularly with a young or novice horse, so avoid doing too much work on small circles.

When working on a circle the horse bends his body to the shape of the circle. The length of the outer, stretched, side of his body will measure a lot more than the inner, rather squashed, side of his body as shown in fig. 85. Because working on a circle stretches and squashes the horse's body (the extent of squashing and stretching depending on the size of the circle) it means that working the horse on a circle makes him more supple along both outside lengths of his body.

Because working on a circle makes the horse's back and hind legs work harder, very often a young or unsupple horse will not go forward energetically. It is understandable and allowable at first. But if the exercise is to be of any use, the horse must be persuaded to do his work on a circle as energetically as he works on a straight line. As the speed of the horse increases, the weight on the inside hind

Fig. 84 The inside hind leg comes right under the body of the horse.

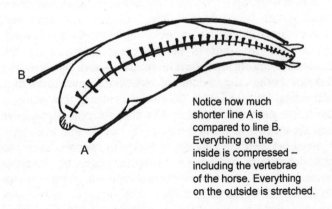

Notice how much shorter line A is compared to line B. Everything on the inside is compressed – including the vertebrae of the horse. Everything on the outside is stretched.

Fig. 85 Working on a circle.

leg increases proportionately and the effort and strain become greater, so once again we must beware of strain.

Working on a circle bends, stretches and supples both sides of the horse's frame. By encouraging the inside hind leg to come under the horse and take more weight it strengthens that hind leg. It also stretches and supples the whole of the top line of the horse including the inside hind leg but not the outside hind leg.

INSIDE LEG OUTSIDE REIN

When you are working a horse his body should nearly always have at least a small amount of bend in it (unless you are working on a totally straight line such as a diagonal or up the centre line). Consequently your aids will normally be those which ask for a bend in the horse's body. That is: inside rein asking for a position to the right, outside rein supporting the inside rein, inside leg on the girth and the outside leg behind the girth keeping the quarters in.

The rider's inside leg will motivate the inside hind leg of the horse to produce forward energy. As the inside hind leg is the most important leg in the movement, coming underneath and taking the weight of the horse, it is important that the rider's inside leg is the most active, motivating the power that will be lifting and carrying the horse. The rider's outside rein, as well as supporting the bend, should be stronger than the inside rein as it is largely responsible for catching and harnessing the energy that comes from the inside hind leg. It is left to the outside rein to perform this task, rather than the inside rein or both of them, because it is essential that the inside rein has a lighter and sometimes mobile contact. If the inside rein had a strong contact the horse would be tempted to use it for support and lean on it rather than take the strong steps that are necessary to balance himself. This is why it is important to ride from the inside leg to the outside hand. The inside leg is providing the energy and the outside rein is containing it. You should see a slight difference in tension between the two reins. The outside rein should be taut whilst the inside rein, though not looped, should have less tension in it.

Some maintain that the inside rein should also be mobile, as described earlier, where the rein is given and taken constantly to a very, very, small degree. This does have the advantage of making the horse aware that he will not be able to lean on the rein, but if this is not likely to be a problem, it doesn't offer any advantage.

To have to keep the rein mobile is more likely to be a nuisance to both yourself and your horse.

Riding in the inside position begins and maintains the process of harnessing the horse's power. To a lesser degree than most exercises it strengthens the inside hind leg and stretches the top line.

RIDING FORWARDS

With rhythm
Working a horse forwards energetically is most important but, before this energy can be asked for, it is essential that your horse develops and maintains rhythm in all his work. The strides of the horse are, or should be, almost musical in their regularity – like the beat of a drum. When you ask your horse to work with greater energy a rhythm must still be maintained – even though it will be a different rhythm. If irregularities appear in the rhythm of his strides, revert to working with less energy and concentrate on regaining and retaining a steady rhythm. When you feel this has become set, gradually increase the energy ensuring that as you do the rhythmic strides survive. Singing or humming while working your horse helps to keep this rhythm in mind and if you have it in your mind there is a better chance that you will convey a sense of it to your horse.

Why do we want to work with energy?
Our ultimate aim when we are schooling a horse is to improve his balance. If you can remember the theory of opposing directional forces – the reins are at the front end controlling the forward movement or speed of the horse while the legs are at the other end generating energy from the hind legs of the horse towards those reins. Imagine again that the horse was a coiled metal spring and imagine that in the

place of the reins was a giant hand pushing against the nose of the horse and restraining it from going too fast. Against the hocks of the horse was another giant hand pushing the horse forwards – making it go faster. You can imagine that if the hands were pushed closer together the frame of the horse would become shorter – it has been squashed together. In order to shorten his outline, his back should lower, his hind legs should come further under him which will automatically raise his forehand. Your legs are in the place of the giant hand on the hocks driving the legs further under the horse. Your reins are in the place of the other hand holding onto the energy, bottling it up inside his frame and not allowing any of it to escape by letting the horse go faster.

You know that if the reins were not restraining or harnessing all this energy the horse would simply stick out his nose and run very fast. His body would appear longer and lower. Like a spring pushed at one end but not held at the other – it would ping off into the distance and become long and loose. If the opposite happened and the reins were ready to hold onto the energy from the hind legs but that energy never materialised, the body of the horse would also remain long and loose. The giant hand on the quarters hadn't pushed at all, leaving the spring uncoiled and floppy and the horse going gently along in the same manner as before. This would be the scenario if there weren't enough energy being generated by the hind legs of the horse. This is why it is so important for us to ride our horses energetically forward – we must provide the energy for the reins to contain so that we are always encouraging our horse to step under his own weight and lift his forehand.

How much energy?

You yourself can imagine just how much a horse's balance is improved by using these two opposing forces. You can see the back legs coming further under the horse and you can see the forehand lift and become more elevated. You can see that as the two opposing forces have started to work they appear to have shortened the outline of the horse – his body has changed shape. It would be nice to think that all you had to do when riding was just to clamp your hands on the reins and kick your horse on enthusiastically to achieve the desired result – but the horse cannot change his shape overnight. When he is a novice he will be neither strong enough nor supple enough so at first you will have to accept a horse whose outline is long and relatively flat. If you were to push this horse forward with a lot of energy the horse would not be able to put his back legs underneath him. The extra energy would push more weight onto the forehand. Even though the horse was working on the bit, because there was so much energy for him to absorb, it would all end up leaning on the reins. The body of the horse needs to be developed so that he is more able to use this extra energy by putting his hind legs further underneath him. All the exercises in this chapter will help him to do this. They will help him stretch, supple and strengthen.

The amount of forward energy you ask the horse to produce must depend on his level of training and how supple and strong he is. Gradually as the horse develops he will be able to lower his back and put his hind legs further underneath him and when this takes place you can ask for more forward energy. This is because his body is more supple and strong and his legs are better able to come under him and take his weight.

Having said the above you should always push the horse forward with as much energy as you feel he can cope with, provided you can contain this forward energy with your reins without feeling that the horse is leaning on them. Always work your horse in this way and always push gently at the frontiers of his ability asking just a little more than he wants to give. As you work, think – energy, energy, energy – and think it rhythmically to help you to remember how important this is also.

Riding the walk energetically

Very often when they are on the bit horses walk rather slowly and don't put their back legs under them. Whether it is stiffness or laziness is difficult to say but whatever the cause the cure is the same. If your horse does not walk out strongly or jogs when you ask him to walk on he is actually being disobedient to your leg. It is easier for him to jog than it is for him to walk properly. You need to use a stronger leg aid to ask him to take longer strides behind. The chances are that initially this will make him jog even more, so instead of doing this while he is on the bit, ride him with very long reins. Encourage him to stretch his neck and his whole outline. In this position it is easier for him to take longer strides behind. Encourage him to walk with more and more energy without letting him trot. If he does trot bring him back to a walk immediately. Give the reins to him again and once more ask him to walk on, by putting your leg on. It may take a while before he realises that when you put your legs on you only wish him to walk more strongly but persevere because he will get the message eventually. Walking like this will get his back legs more activated and will help to supple up his frame.

After you have worked like this for a while ask him to lift up his head and work on the bit as you normally would. Use your legs to ask him to keep walking forward energetically while staying on the bit. He should be able to manage this a little better than he could before. Keep practising the above exercise and before long his walk should be much more forward going, his back should be rounded and his back legs should be coming further under him. His back should also be swinging rhythmically as with each stride he purposefully marches forwards.

Working with energy pushes the back legs of the horse further under him and therefore stretches the whole of the top line including both hind legs.

TRANSITIONS

A correctly executed transition makes the horse step under his body. This stepping under strengthens the hind leg of the horse, as each time he does it he takes some of his weight onto his hind legs. It also stretches the whole of his top line particularly his hind legs. If a transition is to be correct, one strong step should take the horse into the other pace.

Young horses and unschooled horses make transitions gradually from one pace to another. For example, from trot to canter, the horse will gain speed until he naturally breaks into canter. As he does it his frame will be long and at the moment of transition he will almost fall forwards into the canter. In a gradual transition down, say from canter to trot, the horse will be slowed up by a closed rein aid and he will gradually get slower and slower until he collapses into trot. Again his frame will be long and stretched and his weight will be on his forehand as it was in his transition up into canter. The reins, continuously asking for the slower pace, will be supporting the horse until he is ready to drop into it.

In all our training of the horse the aim is always to make the horse step under his own weight so that his hind legs carry a gradually greater proportion of his weight and his forehand becomes lighter. To relate this to the way a human stops or slows: run fairly fast and slow down gradually – do you notice how your feet merely go slower without any great effort. Now run fast and stop suddenly. This time you have to put your feet ahead of you as you plant them on the ground. It is quite an effort and you can feel the weight of your body pushing on your feet as they are braced on the ground. They have come under you and caught your weight. This is how we want the horse to make a downward transition – by putting his back legs underneath him. The aids for all the transitions can be found in Chapter 2. One of the most important factors in a correctly executed transition is that the horse knows the aids and obeys them. This often takes a lot of practising.

I make no apology for repeating that the horse must be on the bit and he must remain on the bit throughout the transition. The horse needs to take a step under his own weight in order to execute the transition properly. When he does this he stretches his top line, as said earlier, particularly the back legs. Because the top line is being stretched the horse will have a desire to lift his head into the air to release the strain. Obviously if he lifts his head like this the transition will not have a beneficial effect – he will have avoided stretching his top line. Therefore the rider will have to insist, by keeping a secure contact on the reins, that he does not do this. If the horse has a stiff back and/or is still finding staying on the bit difficult, have sympathy with him here and give him some leeway– he may not find it easy.

HALF HALT

This, in essence, is the same as a downward transition. You use the same aids i.e. the braced back, the legs and the closed hands. Just as the horse accepts your aids and takes that step underneath him to catch his weight and make the transition down, you cease the aids and ask him to go on. The result is your horse has taken a deep step under him with his hind legs but he hasn't stopped – a casual observer may not have noticed anything had happened. By putting his legs under him he has transferred some of the weight from his forehand to his hind legs. This should help him to go more lightly in front and the pace should subsequently improve. The beauty of this exercise is that it can be used not only as an exercise in itself but to improve the balance and pace of the horse as it is working.

Transitions stretch the whole of the top line including both hind legs. They also strengthen the back legs of the horse.

ROUND AND DOWN

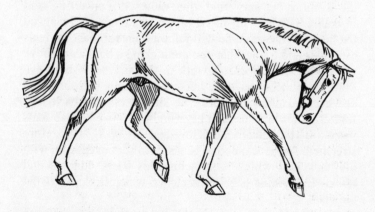

Fig. 86 Round and down.

Round and down is almost the ultimate in stretching exercises. It is, however, only an exercise and not a correct way of going or any kind of classical movement. In this exercise the horse lowers his head while keeping his neck in a rounded outline. To get him working like this it should be possible merely to let out the reins and the horse should lengthen his neck and head until the head is near the ground. Keeping a contact with the reins will keep the horse's neck rounded which in turn will keep the shape of the horse's spine rounded and the back legs coming under him.

Unfortunately the horse may well say he doesn't have the faintest idea what you want of him when you increase the length of rein. If this is the case hold the reins low and ask him to lower his head by gently closing your hands on them – this should give him the idea of what you want. If it does not work you could exercise him on the lunge using a Chambon. This would help to stretch the top line without a rider (which is always easier for the horse) and will show the horse what you mean. If you wish to do the same while riding, use a de Gogue. The horse will find it difficult to maintain his balance in this exercise and will almost certainly fall onto his forehand and rush – he and, more to the point, you may find this rather disconcerting and insecure. The less advanced or the less naturally balanced the horse is, the more he will fall onto his forehand. It feels as a rider and trainer that you are making a backward move when you ask a horse to work in this manner – but have faith. The theory is that, because working in round and down unbalances the horse, he should put his back legs further under him to catch his weight because he also feels insecure. His head is held low and his neck is therefore stretched. At the same time he needs to step under him with his back legs which is stretching his back, quarters and hocks. Everything is being stretched which is exactly what we want.

After a while the horse will be more able to balance when he is working in round and down. He has done this by stretching that top line and stepping further under his weight. This should make improvements in his other work because the top line has been stretched so much by this work. When he resumes his normal working position he should be even more able to balance himself because his hocks should now come further under him.

To work properly in round and down, the outline of the horse should be rounded (as in fig. 86) and not merely stretched out long, low and straight. It is also essential that the rider does not support the horse. The horse must try to find his own balance. If the rider allows the horse to lean on his hands and become the supporting wall then the horse will not put his hocks under to support his weight and will end up remaining on the forehand. If the horse is ridden with a non-supporting contact he has to step well under himself to catch the excessive weight. To do this he lengthens the stride of his back legs and stretches the whole of his frame.

As stated earlier it is quite possible that the horse is initially incapable of stepping under and supporting his weight which does put him on the forehand and will make him rush forward at great speed. Each time he rushes off, bring him back to a slower pace by closing your hands and legs and bracing your back. When he slows up cease the aids – let him carry on as before. Try not to let him lean on your hands or the effect of the exercise will be lost. You can also make it easier for the horse by not asking him to carry his head so low. When he can cope with this position you can then ask him to lower his head further.

Round and down is a particularly useful exercise if you have been working your horse in a collected outline. The shape the horse makes when collected tends to stiffen the frame and reduce elasticity and forward movement. The body of the horse has been squashed together like a spring and if held for long in this position there is a tendency for the work to stick in this coiled position. The work begins to lack elasticity, suppleness and forward movement. By alternating collected work with work in round and down you are relaxing and stretching the metaphorical spring.

There is a justifiable fear that working in round and down makes the horse work on the forehand. Even when the horse has stretched his top line and is coping with the work, the attitude of his body is still placing more weight on his front two legs. It is important therefore to use this as an exercise from time to time and not work in this manner for long periods otherwise the horse may begin to feel at home with this way of going and tend to keep his forehand low in his other work. If you find the work is having this effect, abandon working in round and down until you have corrected the fault with more energetic and collected work. When you return to using the exercise, don't over use it and keep an eye on how it affects his balance. Some horses are naturally more fond of working on their forehand than others and obviously you don't want to encourage them by using this exercise often.

It is possible and useful to do other exercises such as circles, shoulder-in and transitions while the horse is in the round and down position.

Sometimes this exercise is confused with long and low. In the long and low outline the horse merely pokes his nose forward towards the ground and the neck of the horse is quite straight. It is a relaxing exercise but it does not stretch the top line to anything like the same degree.

Round and down stretches the whole of the top line including both hind legs.

LENGTHENED STRIDES (EXTENSION)
Lengthened stride can be performed at walk, trot or canter. As its name suggests, this movement requires the horse to take longer strides. It means the limbs reach out further in each stride so that each step covers more ground than it would normally. How well a horse performs the movement depends on the suppleness of his frame. It also depends upon the freedom of his shoulders – particularly in trot. The front legs pivot from the shoulders and, if there is a natural stiffness or restriction there, the legs cannot swing out to cover more ground. It also depends on how balanced the horse is. If there is too much weight on the front legs they are pinned down by this weight and are only able to take small strides before they have to return to earth again. A horse that is well balanced and taking more of his weight with his hocks will have removed much of the weight from the forelegs, thus allowing him more freedom to move lightly and unencumbered in front.

Walk

To teach a horse to lengthen his walk stride, ask him to walk forward energetically as fast as he can go without breaking into a trot. At the same time allow the reins to lengthen so that he can stretch his frame. Even though you are asking him to go faster now, and you know that ultimately speed is not required, you will find that as well as going faster he is also covering more ground with each stride. Because he is covering more ground he is bringing his back legs further under him and his front legs should be swinging more from the shoulders. He should also have lengthened his frame. You will feel each long stride under you as his back legs are covering more ground. If you were to look behind, you should see his quarters lifting up and down with the stretch of each stride. To start with, you should exaggerate the extension by allowing the horse to stretch his neck as much as he can because this helps him to get the idea of what you want. When he is walking forwards strongly with good long strides, you can gradually reduce the length of the reins, but still keep him working with as much energy and length of stride.

To perform a properly executed lengthened stride in walk, the horse should remain on the bit but be allowed a little extra length of rein so that his head is just a little ahead of the vertical.

Lengthened stride in trot

A horse's ability to lengthen his stride in trot will depend very much on the natural freedom of his shoulder. If the foreleg swings freely from the shoulder he will have little difficulty in increasing the length of his stride. With the novice horse that has a free shoulder, the lengthening may be very exaggerated and will probably be very much on the forehand. If, however, nature has given the horse a shoulder with restricted movement he will find the movement very hard and probably end up merely running faster with relatively short strides.

Initially when you ask the horse to lengthen his stride in trot, just as in walk, allow him to stretch his neck with a longer rein and ask him to trot as fast as he can without cantering. Every so often you will feel him about to break into canter – just close your hands on the reins to stop him doing this. Don't worry that he is dreadfully on his forehand – right now we are only getting him to stretch his frame, loosen his shoulder and activate his hind legs. Keep at it for a few circuits, asking for more and more speed without canter. Have a rest and try again. The shoulder should become freer and the front legs should swing further from the pivot of the shoulder. If the horse is stiff in the shoulder you will need to work on this exercise for some time before you will notice much difference in its freedom. If the horse is very restricted in the shoulder it may never be possible to get much of a lengthened stride because the reason he cannot reach out with his front legs is mechanical. The physical structure of the leg doesn't allow it to pivot forwards. The limit on the horse's extension may be caused by having too much weight on the forehand. In this case this exercise will hardly make any difference to the length of his stride and you may have to wait until you have improved the balance of the horse and until there is less weight pinning the shoulder down.

There is another way to help the horse to take longer strides and this is by using trotting poles. You may already have introduced your horse to trotting poles during his jumping training. If not, look at Chapter 6, page 183, to see how to introduce your horse to trotting poles. Find the right distance for your horse to trot comfortably over the poles (the hind foot of the horse should land approximately half way between the poles) and then increase the distance between each pole by a few inches. Take your horse over them a few times and notice whether this makes him stretch his stride. Have someone on the ground watching him (and adjusting the poles for you!) and looking to see if his stride is lengthening. It should do so but only very slightly. Do the same again and increase the distance by another couple of inches. Take him over them and see how he copes with this distance. If he is capable of lengthening his stride you should begin to notice it. If you feel he can cope with it add another couple of inches to the distance between the poles. Be careful not to make them too far apart as he will begin to put in an extra stride from time to time. It will probably be necessary to ride him over the stretched poles with a little more energy to help him cope with the longer distance. Doing this exercise may help the horse realise what it is you want and rather than running faster he may be able to lengthen his stride.

Remember, though, that your horse may be physically unable to increase the swing of his foreleg from his shoulder. It is much to do with conformation. You may have to wait until later in his training when hopefully he may have a little more freedom in the shoulder. Even if the exercises above have not helped the horse lengthen his stride in front, they will hopefully have helped to activate and strengthen the back legs to some degree and so it should not have been a waste of time.

What you have done so far is stretch the frame of the horse, made him use his hind legs energetically, and increase the ability of the forelegs to swing freely forwards from the shoulder. It is possible that the movement may look extravagant but it will almost certainly be on the forehand. If this is the case the next job to do is teach the horse to restrain himself and only give you a small amount of lengthened stride so that he does not lose his balance. Ultimately the extension needs to come from the power and lifting ability of the hind legs and it is only when the horse has become strong and balanced behind that this will be possible. There is a tendency at this stage, if the horse is capable, to ask him to produce a lengthened stride of too great a magnitude because he can do it – because it is very impressive – but this will almost certainly throw him onto his forehand. As his training progresses and his ability to carry his own weight develops he will gradually be able to put his hind legs further underneath him and still remain balanced even with longer strides in front.

In fig. 87 the horse at the top is lengthening his strides in trot. The horse at the bottom is in ordinary trot. Notice that the head of the horse performing lengthened strides is extended a little further forward than the other horse. When a horse lengthens his strides he stretches his frame and therefore should be allowed to stretch his whole body

Fig. 87
(Top) Lengthened strides.
(Bottom) Ordinary trot.

including his head and neck to achieve the freedom of the movement. If a horse were asked to perform lengthened strides without being allowed to stretch his neck he would be restricted and not able to perform the movement to his best.

Lengthened stride at canter

Lengthened strides at canter are really more lengthened bounds than strides. A horse's ability to perform it well is less to do with the freedom of the shoulder and more to do with the power of the hindquarters. The hind legs come well under the horse propelling it further forwards than normal. Canter lengthened strides are a useful exercise because the surge of power tends to bring the hind legs further under the horse and consequently lighten the forehand.

Lengthened strides stretch the top line, particularly both hind legs. They also help to loosen the shoulder of the horse as he reaches out further with his front legs.

LATERAL WORK

The following exercises would all be described as lateral work because the horse is stepping sideways under his own body. These exercises all strengthen the hind legs as they come under the body of the horse and carry more of his weight. They also make the hind legs and the back suppler as they have to stretch to reach under the horse.

Leg yielding

This is a very simple exercise though in itself it doesn't stretch the horse's frame or improve his balance. Its purpose is to teach the horse to go away from your leg. It is a very easy exercise both for him to do and for you to teach him. He should not find it difficult or stressful. Before you start this exercise you should have spent some time handling your horse and showing him how to move away from your hand on the ground by taking sideways steps. At first do this in the stable by pushing him to one side with your hand in the flank area. When he understands what you mean, begin to ask him to move away from your hand when it is placed nearer to his girth until eventually he will move away from your hand when it is just behind the girth. By practising this from the ground it will help him understand what you want when you are mounted and pushing with your leg.

Initially ask him to go away from your leg while you are mounted but standing still. Try pushing him quite firmly with one leg. If he doesn't go sideways ask someone to push him over for you while you are also pushing with your leg. He should take a step to the side away from the pressure of your leg and the pressure of your assistant's hand. If he does, make a big fuss of him – he has been quite clever. Then use your other leg to push him the other way. Next, do it at walk, again with someone to help push him over if necessary. When he has managed this well on both reins ask for it at trot.

You can also use your weight to help the horse move sideways. Cast your mind back to the discussion on human balance and to the part where a human is carrying a small child on his shoulders (page 24). Because the child leans to one side the human feels the child will fall off or pull him over. To stop this happening the human takes a step underneath the weight of the child. It is an instinctive reaction that the horse shares with us. So if we lean in the direction we want the horse to move, it will make him want to step under your weight to catch it and stop you falling off. When you move your leg backwards to push the horse sideways it is easy to shift your weight from the seat bone of that leg so that most of your weight falls on the opposite seat bone.

Leg yielding can be performed in either walk, trot or canter, though walk and trot are quite sufficient for our needs. The aids for leg yielding are increased pressure from the outside leg behind the girth together with an increase in the rider's weight over the inside hip. The outside rein is slightly shortened and the inside slightly lengthened so that the bend of the horse's body is pointing in the direction he is going. In this position the horse will find it a lot easier to perform the movement. It both looks and feels as if all his weight is on his shoulder and this is pulling him to one side. His head and his legs appear to follow on rather aimlessly. Once the horse has understood that he has to move away from the leg he finds this movement very easy.

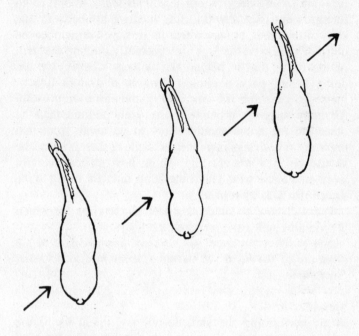

Fig. 88 Leg yielding.

From the angle of the horse's body shown in fig. 88 you can see the reason the horse finds the exercise so physically undemanding. The horse has bent his body at his shoulder leaving the rest of his body travelling in a straight line behind it. His legs are moving under him as they normally do – they do not have to cross under the horse to execute the sideways movement nor do they have to carry any extra weight. Leg yielding is only practised to introduce lateral work. When the horse happily moves away from the leg it is a movement to abandon as it has no effect on the horse's suppleness and strength. It is also teaching the horse a possible evasion.

Teaching the horse to move away from your leg is a very basic part of equitation and this is what this exercise sets out to do. Whenever we are riding the horse, he needs to be listening to and obeying our legs. Our legs ask him to go forwards but they also ask him to move his body to one side, or the other, or stay where he is. If you remember the corridor of power, the legs are constantly guiding that part of the horse that is behind the withers whether we are doing a half pass, a circle, going in a straight line or jumping. Teaching this exercise is, therefore, very useful for many purposes. If one leg exerts more pressure than the other leg the horse should know to go away from that pressure. If both legs maintain the same contact it means he should go in a straight line. Think how difficult correct work on a circle would be if the horse didn't respond to the directional aids of your legs.

We will now go onto other lateral exercises for which leg yielding will have prepared the horse.

Leg yielding produces no physical improvement in the physique of the horse; it merely teaches him to go away from the leg.

Shoulder-in
When performing the shoulder-in, the shoulders of the horse are moved off the track as in fig. 89, while the hind legs stay where they are. The horse is bent as if he was on a circle but he is actually going in a forward direction along the track. Because the front of the horse is off the track, the step of the inside hind leg comes further under the horse's body and takes more of the weight of the horse.

The aids for shoulder-in are similar to those for a circle or bend, that is, the inside rein initiates the bend while the outside rein allows and then limits and supports the bend. Just as with a circle, this is achieved by pivoting the upper body in the direction of the bend. Immediately after the shoulders of the horse have come off the track, both hands should close momentarily on the reins indicating to the horse that you do not wish him to continue on the circle.

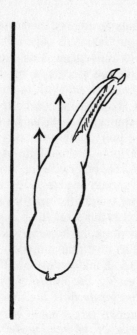

Fig. 89 Shoulder-in.

The inside leg of the rider should have a stronger aid than it would for a circle and it should push the horse in the direction of the movement along the track. The outside leg of the rider keeps the body of the horse in the shape of the bend and stops the quarters from falling out. The weight is transferred to the outside hip in the direction of the movement. The horse will be aware that we are leaning in this direction and will move that way to catch our weight.

As with the circle, the shoulder-in strengthens and stretches the inside hind leg, but even more so because of the angle of the horse and the angle of the step he is taking. He has to step further under him and take more weight than he would on a circle. As he stretches his hind leg he also stretches his back.

In shoulder-in the horse's body is bent in the same way as when he is working on a circle. Hence there is the same stretching of the outside edge of the horse's frame, and the same compressing of the inside edge achieved when working on a circle. The movement is an exaggerated form of working from inside leg to outside hand, and therefore it also encourages the horse to work in the correct position. After working in shoulder-in, the correct flexion for an inside position becomes much easier for the horse.

There should be no reduction in energy when the horse performs shoulder-in – it should be as energetic as the work in a straight line, otherwise the movement would be of less value. You should be able to feel the inside leg as it comes under the horse and lifts him forwards. There should be more of a punch to this stride than any other. If you are unable to feel it, perhaps the horse is working with insufficient energy or at an insufficient angle – you may need to ask him to bring his shoulders further off the track.

Shoulder-in stretches the whole of the top line of the horse including the inside hind leg. Because the horse is stepping under and carrying some of his weight it strengthens this leg. Because of the bend in the body, shoulder-in also stretches the outside edge of the horse and compresses the inside edge.

Travers (or quarters-in)

When working in travers the horse is bent in the same shape as he is in shoulder-in, as in fig. 90, but instead of pushing the shoulders off the track, the quarters are pushed off the track. Again the inside leg has to be placed on the girth so that the horse bends his body around it. The outside leg pushes the quarters of the horse off the track and also asks the horse to go along the track in this shape. The rider should shift his or her weight to the inside seat bone. This time the outside hind leg has to come under the horse and take its weight and therefore it is this leg that will be strengthened. Because the outside edge of the horse is being stretched it will make this edge more supple and elastic.

Because some horses have a tendency to go crooked by swinging their quarters in off the track many believe it is foolish to use this exercise which encourages the horse to do exactly that. However, one of the aims of schooling

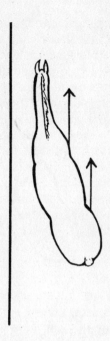

Fig. 90 Travers (head to the wall).

your horse is to have control of the position of the quarters and, if the horse is obeying your leg, keeping his quarters on the track should not be difficult. If you are not completely confident in your ability to do this it would be unwise to use this exercise.

Working in travers stretches the outside edge of the horse and strengthens the outside hind leg.

Renvers (or tail to the wall)

As in the shoulder-in, the forelegs, shoulder and head of the horse are taken off the track. The difference from the shoulder-in is that the horse's body is bent in the totally opposite direction. Rather than being bent to the inside and looking in the direction of a circle, as in the shoulder-in, he is bent to the outside and looking in the direction that he is going. To ask the horse for renvers, push the horse off the

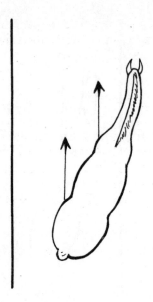

Fig. 91 Renvers (tail to the wall).

track with the outside leg on the girth. The outside rein should ask the horse to create a bend to the outside while the inside leg also asks for the body of the horse to bend to the outside. The inside rein supports and limits the action of the outside rein and is the rein which captures the forward energy of the movement. The rider's weight should be on the inside seat bone, in the direction of the movement, encouraging the horse to step under this weight.

The benefits of this exercise are similar to those of the shoulder-in. It makes the inside hind leg stronger as it steps under the body of the horse and carries more of its weight. That inside hind leg increases in flexibility as well as strength and the top line of the horse is stretched.

Renvers will create a greater improvement in the lateral bend of the horse. Many horses have a tendency to go crooked on a straight line by bringing their quarters in off the track. While the horse is in renvers, you are bending him in completely the opposite way to this crookedness, and therefore you are more likely to correct it and make him go straight.

Full pass

This movement requires the horse to step sideways, only at walk, with no forward movement whatsoever. The outside leg should be behind the girth asking the horse to go sideways – your weight should shift onto the opposite hip just as in leg yielding. When asking the horse to leg yield, his body is bent away from the direction he is going which makes it easier for him. In full pass you should ask the horse for the opposite bend so that the open side of his body is facing the direction he is going. Full pass is not as easy as leg yielding because the horse has to step sideways underneath his body.

Suppose you wish to execute a full pass to the right. The head of the horse should be looking to the right and therefore your right rein will ask him to look that way (supported by your left rein) as if he was turning slightly to the right. Your right leg will be on the girth, keeping the middle of his body concave. Your left leg should be behind the girth asking the horse to move sideways away from that leg and your weight should be on the right seat bone. When the horse steps sideways he has to put his hind leg (the left leg) under his own weight. This stepping underneath his weight helps to stretch and strengthen this hind leg. It is useful to teach this exercise as a prelude to half pass.

Half pass

This is a movement where the horse travels sideways and forwards at the same time. In other words he travels diagonally, as shown in fig. 92. The angle of the diagonal movement can vary. The stronger the angle the harder the half pass is for the horse.

The aids for half pass are the same as for full pass but, because it is performed while the horse is moving forwards either at walk, trot or canter, the movement ends up being diagonal. The horse should be bent as he is in full pass, facing the direction he is going. By using the same aids as

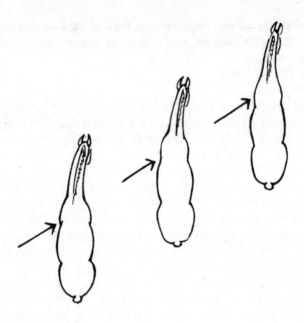

Fig. 92 Half pass.

for full pass the horse should make sideways and forwards steps. The greater the angle of the movement away from the straight line, the greater the bend in the horse's body, and the greater the angle of step the horse has to take under his body with the inside hind leg. To achieve this the rider uses a stronger aid from the outside leg, pushing the horse further in the direction he is going, and asks for more bend with the inside rein. The two aids together create a greater degree of bend in the horse's body.

Executed properly, the horse has to step well under his body as he moves his outside hind leg sideways. This exercise will help to lengthen and strengthen the stride of the hind leg. It will also stretch and strengthen the back of the horse. When the horse steps sideways he steps under his body with his hind leg which, until the other hind leg has changed position, will bear the weight of the horse. The more sideways the step, as against forwards, the further under himself the horse has to step, and therefore the more of his own weight he will be taking on that leg.

SERPENTINES

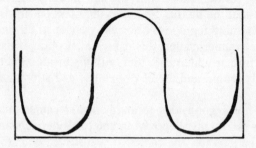

Fig. 93 Serpentines.

Riding a serpentine is putting three or more half circles together. It is of no more value from an exercise point of view than an ordinary circle, but it is a good test of the obedience of the horse and of his flexibility. It is also a good test for the rider who must, on the centre line, change the aids from a bend on one rein to a bend on the other.

When riding a serpentine each half circle should take the horse onto the track at the side of the arena. Make sure, when changing from one half circle to another, that there is a clear difference of bend in the horse's body. On the centre line for a moment the horse should be ridden absolutely straight.

Counter canter (false canter)
While cantering on a circle the horse finds it easier to balance himself if the inside foreleg is leading. This is because at the same time as the inside foreleg comes further forward so does the inside hind leg and in doing so carries the extra weight that the inside hind always carries when working on a circle.

If we ask the horse to canter with the outside fore leading (counter canter), the outside hind would want to follow the sequence and come further forwards than the inside hind. But this will make it difficult for the horse to balance himself. He will naturally want to bring his inside hind leg further under him so that this leg can take the weight that being on a circle imposes on it. Because the inside hind leg doesn't normally come so far under the horse in counter canter, this exercise encourages the horse to step further underneath him with his inside hind than he normally would and thereby stretches and strengthens this leg.

It is not a good idea to start counter canter until your horse is thoroughly happy with and totally understands and obeys the aids for true canter. If you started counter canter too soon the horse would easily become very confused.

The aids for counter canter on the right rein are the aids for left canter and vice versa, but when you first ask the horse for counter canter start in true canter. Canter first in a straight line. Gradually bring the horse off the straight line as shown in fig. 94. At first, the maximum the horse should be away from the track is about a metre. Ask him to come off the straight line by asking a little more with the inside rein and pushing his body off the track with your outside leg. To return him to the track use your inside leg and outside rein. It is essential to keep your body and legs in the same position so that he knows you want him to keep this canter. He will find this movement easier if at first he is not asked to bend his body in the direction he is going and, as shown in fig. 94, retains the existing bend in his body.

Gradually, as the horse becomes more supple and strong, you can make the loop of counter canter deeper and ask him to bend his body more in the direction of the bend. After the horse has mastered the loop of counter canter he can be asked to canter around the short side of the arena in counter canter. To do this, start in true canter and cross the arena diagonally so that he will be approaching the short side in counter canter. Allow him to cut the corner of the short side slightly so that the movement is easier for him.

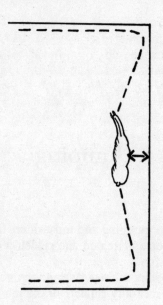

Fig. 94 Counter canter.

6

Jumping

Most horses like jumping and most riders like jumping – it is fun. If the horse is trained and ridden properly it should always remain fun.

Before schooling a horse over jumps, the rider must be physically and mentally capable of the job. He or she must have a strong, supple, balanced and independent seat which means the reins must not be relied on for any support whatsoever (see Chapter 2 on Better Riding). If a rider has never schooled a horse to jump, it is as well to be taught first how to ride over jumps on a horse that is well established in his jumping.

The jumping seat is different from the normal riding seat. Firstly you must shorten your stirrup leathers by two holes. This will place your weight slightly more forward over the shoulders of the horse and it will increase the amount of bend in your knees and ankles. Your length of rein should also shorten as you bring your body forward nearer to the horse's head but there must still be a straight line from your elbows down the reins to the horse's mouth. It is important that, as the horse takes off over the jump, you maintain a contact with his mouth that is constant yet sympathetic. When the horse jumps he needs to be able to stretch his entire frame. The amount he stretches his body will depend on the height and the width of the jump. As he stretches, you must be careful to allow this stretching, by going forward with the horse over the jump and stretching your body, arms and fingers to allow the head of the horse to go as far forward as he needs to negotiate the jump. As you stretch forward, keep some weight on the stirrups and keep the angle of your lower leg the same i.e. hanging straight down and not thrown up in the air on the horse's flank or pushed forwards on his shoulder.

If you don't go forward with the horse you may well 'catch' him in the mouth as he jumps and stretches. This will hurt him and make him lose confidence – he will not want to repeat the experience and may not want to jump again. As the horse stretches, the rider should be aware of the horse's head reaching forwards and should follow this movement with his or her hands. The hands should not go forwards suddenly but should be taken forward by the horse. As the horse lands, the reverse should happen and the rider should gradually contract the fingers, arms and body and revert to the normal riding position as the horse shortens his frame. If you do not do this you will be on the landing side of the jump with long, looping reins. The horse will have no contact or direction from you. The horse needs to know what to do and where to go next and if you have no contact with the horse through the reins he will know you have let go of him. It is a very unnerving experience for a horse and can cause him to lack the confidence to jump again. If you have no contact with the reins it also means that you are unable to collect, balance or turn your horse ready for another jump.

It is most important for you to have the right attitude towards jumping. You must be keen and not in any way frightened of the consequences of jumping even if it all goes wrong and you end up in a heap on the ground. If you are frightened, nervous or tense the horse will instantly know and will presume that the reason for your fear is associated with the jump.

The horse also must be physically and mentally ready to learn to jump. He should at least be obedient to the rider's leg and rein aids, and be able to achieve a degree of leg yielding on either rein. He should be able to perform in all three paces calmly and obediently, including working correctly on a 20 metre circles in all paces. He should be able to perform all transitions calmly and obediently and he

Fig. 95 Jumping.

should be reasonably well balanced and not leaning on the rider's hand. The schooling over jumps can then be gradually brought into the flat work. Jumping is an extension of the other work and should not be practised in isolation as if it were an entirely different discipline. The flat work should always be an integral part of the jumping work.

A horse's first introduction to jumping comes when you ask him to walk over a heavy pole on the ground. It should be at least 10cm (4 inches) in diameter and approximately 2.75 metres (9 feet) long. Ideally this pole should be placed at right angles to and somewhere near a hedge, wall or fence. This will give a young horse a feeling of security. Ideally it should also be placed between two wings (without cups) and facing the direction of home. As shown in fig. 96 the initial approach should begin from the opposite direction followed by a smooth arc, bringing the horse to a position where he faces the centre of the pole. You must then walk him in a straight line over the centre of the pole. He should walk slowly, calmly and smoothly without altering rhythm or balance. After he has done it praise him.

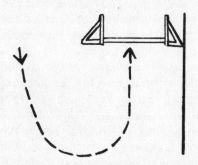

Fig. 96 Begin the approach from the opposite direction.

Approximately one horse in every 20 or so may not want to go over the pole. If your horse is one of these, and looks at it as if it were a snake on the ground, do not become cross with him. Remember that he is probably fearful of it so do not punish him for not going over it – this will only add to his fear. If your horse is obedient to your leg aids, place your legs on his sides, quietly insisting that he goes over the pole. Make a big fuss of him when he goes over it, ignoring the manner in which he accomplishes it. If necessary get another horse or a person to give you a lead. Next ask him to go over the pole three or four times in both directions, praising and rewarding him. After this either stop work or go onto something else. The next three or four times you work him do the same.

By doing this you:

A.   Let your horse know there is nothing frightening about a pole on the ground.

B.   Let him know that he must obey you when you ask him to go over it and

C.   Keep it fun by not punishing him, and praising and rewarding him when he goes over it.

Next the horse should trot over the pole. Again approach the centre of the pole in a straight line, calmly trot over it and then praise him. Do this several times on each rein.

After your horse is happily going over the pole on the ground in trot, it is time to replace it with a small cross poles jump. It should be no more than 30cm (12 inches) high. Approach it out of trot in exactly the same manner that you approached the pole on the ground. Keep him calm and quiet as he approaches the jump and goes over it. Don't forget to go forward with your body and your hands as the horse jumps and don't forget to praise him after he has jumped. Work the horse over the jump several times on both reins before you progress to the next stage. Do not go on to the next stage until your horse is jumping calmly.

If your horse has been well schooled he should go forwards from your legs when you squeeze them against his side. There should be no need to kick him. The same applies when you are jumping. If he doesn't go forwards when you put your legs on gently, increase the pressure of your legs. If this doesn't work, rather than kicking him use your jumping stick just behind your leg. It should be sufficient just to tickle him with it. If he still doesn't go forwards from your leg, perhaps you had better return to your work on the flat, until he learns to listen to your leg and to go forwards when you increase the pressure.

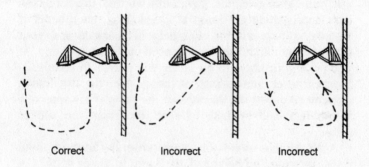

Correct   Incorrect   Incorrect

Fig. 97 The approach.

The approach you make to the jump is very important. It must be at the centre of the jump and it must be at right angles to it. You must not try to jump it from an angle. Fig. 97 shows the right way to do it and two common errors. It is not a good idea to approach the jump from a long distance away in a straight line. If you do, the horse may get tense in anticipation and may rush the fence or possibly have time to decide to be frightened of it and set up evasions of one sort or another.

In the last three strides before the jump the horse needs to be left alone to sort out the jump for himself. It is important during this time not to kick him, hit him, shorten your reins, shift your position or do anything else which might disturb his concentration. The only thing which you do as you approach the jump is to keep your legs against the side of the horse. Don't take your legs off before you go over the jump, (this would probably make him think you didn't want to go over it). Keep them on, and keep on squeezing him to encourage him over the jump. If you feel him go forward from your leg, this pressure will not need to be very great. If, however, you feel he is backing off from your leg (that is, not going forward when you put them on), increase the pressure of your legs. The horse will not find this distracting because it is merely a continuation of what you were doing earlier. Don't be worried if your horse isn't approaching the jump at speed. It is much better if he goes slowly as this will help his balance and your control. Not all horses need speed in order to jump. If you push your horse to go faster you may well unbalance him and teach him to rush at fences. He will also find it difficult to gauge the distance of the jump if his approach is too fast, and he may take off too soon, too late or refuse.

After he has done this jump several times on both reins, increase the height of the jump to about 45cm (18 inches). Leave the cross poles and add a pole going straight across behind the poles and another on the ground on the approach side of the jump. The cross poles focus the horse's sight on the centre of the jump and also provide a fuller jump. Horses, particularly young ones, do not like jumping gappy or open jumps or jumps with thin poles. They also find it easier to work out the position of a jump if there is a pole on the ground at the foot of the jump. The jump must be inviting for the young horse. Because this jump is small you can still jump it out of trot remembering to keep the horse calm and quiet. If you wish you could let him canter to the jump as long as this does not upset his calmness and balance. If you wish to jump this from the other direction remember to rebuild the jump so that it faces the horse as he takes off. In other words the ground line pole should be on the ground nearest to the horse and the straight pole should be behind the cross poles. It is very important that jumps should be made this way round because the horse judges the jump from the ground line. If the ground line was further away than the rest of the jump it would seriously confuse him and his take off. If there is a ground line it must be that part of the jump that is closest to the horse when he takes off. Parallel jumps, planks and gates have no ground line.

Gradually increase the size of the jumps until they are about 75cm (2 feet 6 inches) high and wide and he is jumping them confidently and with ease. If at any stage in his training he gets upset or tense or makes a mistake go back a stage in his training to a point where he finds it really easy. If your horse rushes the jumps try to calm him down rather than pin him down. If you take too strong a contact on the reins he may become worried that he is not going to be able to stretch over the jump and he may refuse it. Do any slowing down that is necessary before the last three strides. After this, you have to let him find his own pace. If he still rushes take him back to a pole on the ground or very small jumps and try to get him in the habit of going calmly again.

When introducing horses to jumping you have to be very careful to progress slowly. They should always regard the jumping as fun and as easy. Try to make it so that they never want to refuse a jump, because it is so easy for them. If for some reason your horse does refuse, always presume there was some reason other than disobedience for the refusal and don't get cross. He will remember your anger for ever and may always associate pain, discomfort or unhappiness with jumping. Keep the whole thing fun. If he has refused a jump make it smaller or easier or think of another way of asking him to do it that he won't find as hard.

Resist the temptation to test your horse to see how high he can jump just because he seems to find it easy. Very gradually increase the height and the width of jumps – never let him have an excuse to refuse and never, ever, risk over facing him. If he makes a mess of it and hurts himself he will remember it for a long time.

After your horse is easily jumping small plain obstacles, it is a good idea gradually to introduce different types of jumps such as hedges, coloured poles and fillers. Make sure they are all very small so that he can easily see over the other side of the jumps and knows that he can jump them. Introduce the different jumps one by one and on different days so that you don't faze him with a lot of new experiences.

Sometime around now you could introduce your horse to a small double. The easiest double is one with two non-jumping strides. The first element should be the cross poles with a pole behind and in front that you jumped earlier. The second element should ideally be an upright jump such as a horizontal pole set at about 45cm (18 inches) with a pole on the ground immediately in front of the jump and a diagonal pole from the end of one pole to the ground. The distances between the two jumps will vary according to the height and stride of your horse. At this stage in the training it is very important to help your horse get his jumping right by finding out his normal length of strides between jumps. The average would be 9.15 metres (30 feet) when you approach the first part of the combination in trot. The horse would then make two canter bounds between the fences before taking off for the second element. The distance between would be greater for a horse and less for a pony. Get someone on the ground to watch him jumping to make sure that the distance is right for him. If you were to approach this jump in canter the distances between the jumps should be slightly greater i.e. approximately 10 metres (33 feet).

Placing poles
Once your horse is jumping well and confidently you could introduce him to placing poles. They help both horse and rider see the take off point for the jump, and help train their eye for all jumping. They also help to improve the rider's feel of rhythm and ability to judge distances and 'see a stride'. If you are trotting over the jump the placing pole should be approximately 2.4 – 2.75 metres (8 – 9 feet) in front of the jump. If you are intending to canter over the jump, the pole should be approximately 6.1 metres (20 feet) from the jump. According to the horse's actual take off these poles can be moved nearer or further away from the jump. If he gets too close to the jump, pull the pole further away from it. But if he is standing too far back from the jump move the pole closer.

Trotting poles

You will have already trotted your horse over one pole. Again place a pole on the ground somewhere on the track of your arena or work area and trot your horse over it in rising trot. (You should always be in rising trot over trotting poles.) He should go calmly over it. After you have done this, add another pole approximately 2.75 metres (9 feet) from the first pole. Again approach the centre of the poles in a straight line and trot calmly over them. Praise him. Do not allow him to canter over them. It may be necessary to adjust the distance between the poles depending on the size of your horse's strides. If the horse has to reach to go over the second pole reduce the distance accordingly. If he is a little on top of the second pole when he is about to step over it, increase the distance. The second pole should lie somewhere in the centre of the horse's take off and landing points. When you have got the right distance add another pole the same distance apart as shown in fig. 98 and trot over all three. Praise him. Gradually add one or two more poles at the same distance apart. Ride up and down the poles on both reins. Keep him calm and praise him. Very often a horse will look down at the poles, lower his head and round his back as he goes over them. This turns the trotting poles into a good stretching exercise. The exercise also makes the horse use his back legs and encourages his co-ordination both mental and physical. The trotting poles would initially be placed on the ground but, after he is working up and down them happily, they could be lifted up a few inches, perhaps using blocks of wood at either end of the pole.

When the horse and rider are more confident and balanced, progress from these distances to closing each of the gaps one by one until they are placed at approximately 1.4 metre (4 feet 6 inch) intervals. A young horse or novice rider can easily become unbalanced, lose rhythm and become frightened if the poles were to be put at this distance before being ready.

It can help the horse to steer a straight course into the poles (at either distance) if another pole or poles are laid on the ground at right angles on the approach to them, and at

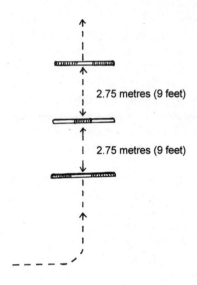

Fig. 98 Trotting poles.

the far end, as shown in figs. 99 and 100.

Grid work
The horse should be proficient in his trotting pole work and jumping small jumps happily before you introduce him to jumps of any height. It is also useful to work him over combinations of jumps. This will improve his stamina, his strength, his flexibility and his eye. It will also help you to develop your own co-ordination and eye and the confidence and suppleness of both you and your horse.

It is essential to have someone on the ground helping you to add poles and move jumps. This is most difficult to do on your own. It would be preferable to have someone helping you who is experienced at jumping.

Initially lay down four trotting poles on the ground at the correct distance for your horse. Trot over them several times, accustoming your horse to them. After this, put up a cross poles jump of about 60cm (2 feet) high and 2.75 metres (9 feet) from the last trotting pole. Trot along the

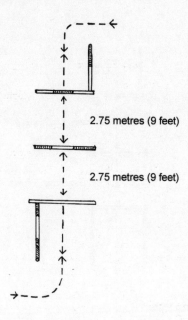

2.75 metres (9 feet)

2.75 metres (9 feet)

Fig. 99 A pole at right angles.

trotting poles and jump the first jump out of trot.

The second jump should be approximately 5.4 metres (18 feet) from the first jump. It should be slightly wider and higher than the first jump. This distance will allow the horse to put in one non jumping stride between the first and second jump. It is only approximate, and at this stage of gymnastic jumping it is better to alter the distances so that they exactly suit your horse. Again approach the trotting poles. Trot over them, jump the first jump out of trot and allow the horse a canter bound between the jumps and then over the second jump.

The third jump could have two non jumping strides and its approximate distance would be twice as great.

After your horse has enjoyed these three jumps a few times you could alter the distance between the first two jumps to a bounce. In a bounce jump the horse takes no non jumping strides between the jumps and takes off

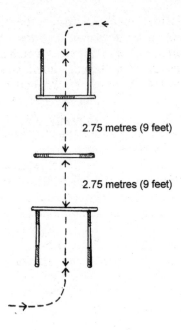

2.75 metres (9 feet)

2.75 metres (9 feet)

Fig. 100 Two poles at right angles.

immediately he lands. The distance here will be approximately 3 metres (10 feet) as he will be jumping out of trot. If you remove the trotting poles and jump the bounce out of canter the distance should be approximately 3.8 metres (12 feet 6 inches). If you are asking the horse to jump over a bounce fence that is over 75cm (2 feet 6 inches), it should always be out of canter, never trot. If you are asking the horse to jump a bounce fence you should not use a placing pole before the first jump.

When working a young horse over grids it is not a good idea to make the last fence of the line a parallel. It is harder for the horse to judge a parallel and by the time he has come to the end of a line of jumps there is a fair chance that he may be struggling. He may not be able to cope with it, either refusing or hurting himself. It is very important to avoid nasty experiences.

When you first start athletic jumping you will place the

jumps at a distance apart which suits the horse. When the horse becomes more proficient at it you can increase his ability by shortening some distances which makes him take shorter bounds, and lengthening others which makes him stretch his strides. A longer bound will make the horse reach for his jumps and flatten. A shorter bound makes the horse shorten his strides and makes his jump rounder and higher. The amount you shorten or stretch the distances would only be by about 10 per cent.

If the distance between the jumps is greater, then it will help the horse increase the length of his stride if you ride him at the fence with a little more speed. Conversely if the distance is reduced it will help your horse to shorten his stride if you approach the jump a little more slowly.

It is worth noting now that a horse going downhill at a jump or series of jumps will take longer strides and conversely a horse going uphill will take shorter strides. The strides will also be shorter if the ground is soft and the going is consequently heavy.

Related distances

Before you ride a show jumping course you will need to walk it, both to judge the size and type of obstacles and also to plan the approach you will take with your horse to each of the jumps. You should already know the standard length of your horse's strides between fences. As you walk around the course you will imagine yourself riding your horse and taking the line and approach which you think will suit him best. On that line you will stride the distance between each fence. The average person's stride is approximately 90cm (3 feet). Work out what your normal stride is and, bearing this in mind, work out how many strides your horse will be taking between each jump and whether this will put him in a good position for take off. If you find the distances are either a little short or a little long you will need to take some action when you ride the course to correct this. It may be possible for you to change your track slightly so that you have a greater or a lesser bend in your route, and hence increase or decrease the distance. When you are deciding on your new route, stride the distances again to make sure you have got it right. It may be impossible to change the distance by riding a different route. If the distance is too long for your horse's strides, increase the speed and encourage your horse to take longer strides. If the distance is too short, ride him with less speed, encouraging him to take shorter strides. When he arrives at the jump this will help him be in a good position for take off. When you are striding the distances remember to look ahead at the next obstacle, not at your feet. If you look down, your strides will become shorter.

Take account of the width of the jump and the height of the jump as you are walking the course. A wide jump needs more speed than a narrow jump in order to allow the horse to soar through the air. A high, upright jump needs a lot of collection, which is slow contained energy, so that the horse can ping up and over the jump.

Cross country fences

Next you may want to introduce your horse to cross country jumps and this is not so easy. You can hire many cross country courses to get your horse used to the fences but most of the jumps are rather big or difficult. Some courses do have small fences but most of them are not really suitable to start off a truly novice horse. They are designed for horses a stage further on. They are also away from home, and that in itself is enough to make most horses tense. Ideally you need tiny versions of all the jumps at home, where you can take your time introducing him calmly to all the different types of obstacles. Here your horse will be relaxed and confident in his surroundings. You need to build a post and rails, a hedge, a small drop, a water jump and a tiny ditch. Also a log placed on the ground makes a very inviting jump.

Most horses find post and rails, logs, hedges and drops easy and not at all frightening as long as they are kept small. Unfortunately many horses find water and ditches very frightening. This is almost certainly because their natural instincts tell them to beware of both of them because they may contain something dangerous which they are unable to see. It is as well to presume that your horse will fall into this category and proceed very, very slowly. What you want to avoid is a confrontation which you won't win. You want to put your horse in a situation where he isn't frightened and where, if at all possible, you know you will be able to get him to do as you ask with the minimum of fuss.

First, *water*: the size has to be great enough, front to back, to make the horse put his feet in it without thinking he can jump over it from a walk. It also has to be wide enough, from side to side, to stop the horse from side stepping it easily. Ideally the edges of the water will be fenced so that it is impossible for him to go round it. It can help if the water lies on ground that he is familiar with and often goes across. The best training water jump I made was on a pathway between the paddock and the stable. I hollowed the ground a little and put the hose pipe on it. None of the horses worried about it and happily sploshed through it back and forth. The main thing is to get them to realise that water isn't really that bad. A young, nervous or inexperienced horse will benefit if given a lead through water by a horse that will go straight through it. After he has thoroughly acquainted himself with water, you need to find or create a different water jump. Again look for something easy to go straight through. Perhaps you could build a larger version of the above in the field. Avoid confrontations – only put him at what you think he will go through. Try and find as much water as you can so that he realises there really is nothing to it. Don't ask him to go through water with a difficult approach unless you are sure he will go through it. It is also important to be able to insist that he goes through it just in case you get it wrong and he doesn't want to go through. One time I was out on a mare who really didn't want to go into the water. The only way I could get her through was to turn her round and reverse her through it. This way she didn't see what was frightening her. When she found the water was all right she was prepared to walk through it forwards!

Remember, as always, to make a big fuss of him when he goes into the water. From time to time it is necessary to remind the horse that water is easy, particularly just before doing a cross country competition.

Ditches: If you have a manege you can hollow out a groove to make a very small ditch. Make it about 15cm (6 inches) deep, 2.75 metres (9 feet) from side to side and about 30cm (1 foot) from front to back. This should frighten no horse. He should be able to see the bottom of it easily and that there are no snakes or monsters in it. He should go over it happily. If you are able to, gradually make the ditch a little wider and a little deeper. If you haven't got a manege, perhaps you can do the same in your field (if it is your field!). When riding a ditch you should not look down at it and neither should your horse. Ride the horse forwards boldly over it.

Don't take your horse for a practice around a cross country course until he is jumping at least 75cm (2 feet 6 inches) at home without a problem and be sure that the jumps there are suitable for your horse.

It is easy to get fraught if your horse is nervous jumping over cross country jumps, but remember that it is up to you to make the horse calmer by your attitude, and not to react badly if he is too frightened to do a jump. It is essential, particularly in these early stages, to make the jumping fun and neither scold the horse nor lose your temper (though this latter part is always essential). Ideally you should know that he will always be able to cope with any jump you put him at, but, horses being what horses are, sometimes you, or he, will get it wrong. If there is no reason why he should refuse, put him at the jump again – do not take him too far away and ride him strongly at it. Do not allow yourself to become tense or angry with him and don't turn the refusal into a huge drama. If he doesn't do it the second time there must be some reason – either the jump is frightening him or his training hasn't prepared him well enough. Gracefully go on, or return, to jumps that he is happy with and finish on a good note. Go home and prepare him some more. Perhaps he needs to learn to go better from your leg or perhaps you need to introduce him to that type of obstacle at home.

PROBLEMS

These almost always happen when the correct early training has not been followed – in other words they have been caused through rider error. If this is the case the horse should go back to the beginning in his training over jumps.

It is possible, however, that the horse has developed a bad back, he may have hurt himself jumping or he may be one of those horses who really doesn't like jumping through no fault of the rider. Remember, when you are trying to assess the reason for your horse's problem, that all horses are individuals and what may not spook one horse may spook another, and what one horse will like and take to, another may not. Remember also that horses have incredible memories. There may be something which happened in the past which affects their attitude to what you are doing now.

The main problems are:

Rushing

The reasons for this are:

The horse is too weak to take off using the strength of his hind legs – he needs the lifting power of speed and the impulsion that speed gives him. To correct this, return to your work on the flat and develop the strength of his hind legs. Trotting poles may help him.

The horse is on the forehand. Again you need to return to flat work and develop his balance and the carrying power of his hind legs.

The horse wishes to evade the rider's leg aids. He deliberately goes fast to dissuade the rider from using his or her legs. When the rider does use the legs he will probably ignore them. Again back to flat work. The horse needs to be taught to respect the leg aids.

The rider is using too much leg and has too soft a contact with the reins. Here the rider needs more tuition on the flat.

Fear or tension. It could be the horse is frightened of the jump and this will often make him rush it. Tension often causes extra speed. In this case make the jumps easier and try to keep him calm. Sometimes this fear is caused by a rider who takes too strong a hold on the reins making the horse fearful of not being able to stretch his head and neck over the jump.

Grid work can help a horse to slow down over jumps but if his rushing is caused by any kind of fear or confusion it could have an adverse effect.

It is not always a good idea to put a stronger bit on a horse who rushes over jumps because there may be other reasons for the rushing. If you immediately put a stronger bit on the horse you may frighten him even more because he may think you will not give him his head when he actually jumps. The only horses that need stronger bits over jumps are those that go too fast the whole time. If the rushing is only associated with actual jumping keep the bit the same and solve the problem another way.

Refusing and stopping

The rider interferes with the horse during the last three strides, distracting the horse and putting him off his jump. During these last three strides the rider should sit still and do nothing but encourage the horse over the jump with his or her legs so that the horse can be allowed to concentrate on his jump.

A frightened horse or a cowardly horse. What he sees may frighten him or he may have been badly treated when jumping in the past. The horse needs to be given confidence. The jumps need to be made lower and easier. He needs to be made to realise that nothing is going to hurt him.

The horse arrives at the fence in the wrong position for take off. Try using a placing pole.

The fences are the wrong distance for the horse's stride. Work out the correct distance for your horse between related obstacles and correct the spacing of the jumps. If you are unable to do this (as in a competition), ride your horse so that he will meet the fences right. E.g. if the distance is too great, allow your horse to stretch his body more and to approach the jump with a little more speed. If it is too tight, collect your horse into a shorter outline so that his bounds are shorter.

The jump is too big for the horse's abilities. If you gradually increase the height of the jump you will know when you are approaching his limits. Don't go too near these limits or try to stretch them. Keep him jumping happily within his ability. If you develop the horse's athletic abilities he should be able to jump higher. Working on the flat to improve his balance combined with grid work should develop his suppleness and strength.

A frightened rider. There is nothing more likely to put a horse off jumping than a rider who doesn't have the confidence to jump. The horse always knows, and then becomes frightened of the jump himself. Added to this, the nervous rider tends to ride incorrectly and give wrong signals to the horse. It could be that the rider is lacking confidence because he or she is not strong enough in the seat. Or perhaps the training has been rushed and the rider has been over faced. If the rider is of a nervous disposition perhaps he or she would be better sticking to flat work. It is possible a person like this may never have the courage to jump horses successfully. If the training is at fault then it needs correcting by going back to the beginning by working on the flat to improve the seat and then training over small jumps with an expert trainer.

The rider is not riding positively enough or hesitates when giving the aids. This will make the horse lose confidence. A rider needs to ride positively and assertively. It is a problem often associated with apprehension in the rider. The solution is as above.

An undisciplined horse. He shouldn't have started jumping in the first place. Take him back to his flat work until he learns to behave.

Slippery, hard or poor ground. This will frighten the horse as he feels he may fall or be unable to get a good hold on the ground for a take off. Putting studs in your horse's back feet will help him.

A horse sickened of jumping. Some children jump on and on and on and the ponies often get really sick of it particularly if the pony is old, tired or the ground is hard.

Rider leans forwards too soon and unbalances the horse. *Rider leans forwards too late* and catches the horse in the mouth – this hurts the horse and he doesn't wish to jump again. With both of these last two the rider needs tuition on how to ride over jumps.

The horse may have a sore back. If his back is sore it will be impossible for him to stretch over the jump. It may also hurt him as he moves or jumps. There are more and more horse chiropractors now who are expert at diagnosing and curing damaged backs. The back could also be sore because of an ill fitting saddle.

The rider may be out of balance on the saddle. If the rider had too much weight to one side it would unbalance the horse and he would probably run out to the side of the jump in his efforts to correct the inbalance.

The rider may not be approaching the fence correctly. See earlier description of correct approach.

The rider may be over riding the horse at the jump. The rider is pushing the horse unnecessarily, making the horse go too fast and pushing him onto his forehand. The horse then doesn't have the time to work out the jump and is also too unbalanced.

The horse could be tired.

The rider may be 'dropping' the horse over the fence. This happens when the rider doesn't keep the contact with the reins over the jump and the landing horse has no direction or control from the rider. It tends to make the horse insecure and fearful of jumping – he feels he is on his own.

The horse is being held down on the bit on the approach to the jump before he is ready. A horse needs to know that he is going to be able to stretch his frame sufficiently over the jump.

The horse has been jumped in a standing martingale which has hurt and/or frightened him and he associates pain with jumping. This horse needs to return to jumping small jumps which require only a little stretching of his body – he will know he can cope with these. Gradually increase the height and width of the jumps making sure that he is allowed free movement with his head and neck. Eventually he will have confidence that jumping no longer hurts him.

The horse is in a round and low outline and is unable to see the top of the jump. The horse needs to be able to see all of the jump in order to assess his approach and his jump. The horse should be allowed to hold his head where he is comfortable when he is jumping, particularly during those last three strides.

Running out

If the horse is escaping at the side of the jump it means two things. Firstly he doesn't want to jump the jump. You need to find out why this is and address it. All the reasons above could be reasons why a horse runs out. He should regard jumping as fun and want to jump. What has gone wrong? Secondly he is not obeying both your leg and rein aids. Read again about the corridor of power in Chapter 2 page 63.

When a horse runs out he doesn't usually turn his head in the direction in which he is running out. He will usually keep looking at the jump while bending his body at the shoulder and running sideways around the edge of the jump. You need to straighten his body to keep him to the jump. To do this, turn the horse's head a little towards the direction in which he is running out and put the leg on that side onto his flank as shown in fig. 101. Reinforce the leg aid by holding the whip on that side of the horse. These aids combined should make the horse go in a straight line towards the jump.

Throwing the head in the air

This is usually caused by a fear in the horse that he won't be allowed to stretch himself over the jump. The culprit is usually a rider with a strong hand and/or a strong bit or a rider that has caught the horse in the mouth over the jump. Horses that are stiff along their top line usually suffer more with this because they need every bit of freedom they can get. After a period of time working on the flat the spine/top line is stretched and made more supple and they are more confident in their ability to stretch over the jump. A rider with softer, allowing hands will help give this horse more confidence as he approaches the jump. The horse will then

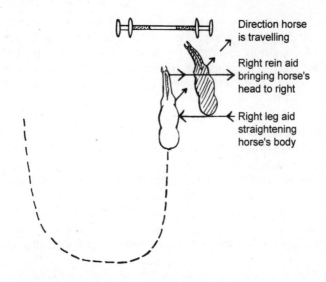

Fig. 101 Aids to prevent running out.

come to trust that the rider will allow the horse to stretch and therefore not fight so hard before the jump to get a longer length of rein.

Cat jumping

Cat jumping is where the horse stops or almost stops at the jump and then lacking momentum springs over the jump like a cat.

The horse is uncertain about the jump and/or the take off. By leaving it until the last moment he can get to a position where he can study the jump before he makes the decision to jump. It is possible that he is cat jumping because he has difficulty in deciding where his take off should be. A placing pole may help him take off at the correct place and may help him train his eye to the correct take off point in future jumping.

Horse is not going forwards into the jump. This could be because the rider has interfered with the horse or is using insufficient leg aids.

196

7

Collection and Working Through

Collection could be described as the opposite to extension. It is a balanced horse moving slowly forwards with great energy. Instead of taking long stretched steps you ask the horse to take short steps. Instead of allowing the energy to propel the horse forwards you want the energy to lift the horse so that he moves forwards, with powerful, cadenced strides. It is important to remember that there should be much energy in collection and, though the forelegs do not cover much ground, the hind legs should come well under the horse to take more of his weight. This transference of weight should lift the front of the horse off the ground and he should go lightly and freely. You should see no weight in the footfalls of his forehand when the horse is collected.

A horse cannot achieve collection until his training has strengthened his hind legs sufficiently to carry more of his own weight nor until the frame of the horse has become sufficiently stretched and supple so that his hind legs are free to come well under him. This suppleness will allow his body to be compressed into a shorter, more elevated attitude.

When the horse is ready for collection use a series of half halts to make the horse step further under his own weight with his back legs but cover less distance with his front legs. Make your leg and back aids stronger so that he should realise you want him to be energetic. At first he thinks you are talking Double Dutch to him – your back and legs seem to be telling him to go faster but your hands

197

are telling him to slow down. If he is used to the aids for the half halt he should have an inkling of the idea. Asking for collection is rather like asking for a half halt where, instead of asking the horse to continue as before, you ask him to make more of those deep steps that he only made one or two of in the half halt. Don't be surprised if he struggles to understand what you mean for quite a while, after all it makes little sense to a lot of humans when asked to ride the movement, never mind the horses. Little by little though the horse will realise what you mean and as the rest of his work progresses he will gradually be able to achieve more and better collection. The exercise is a strain on the hind legs so don't ask for much or for more than a few strides at first. Don't ask for collection at all until your horse is working strongly and confidently in all his work and is happily accepting the action of the bit. Don't ask for any amount of collection until the horse has developed strength and flexibility in the hind leg and strength and flexibility throughout his body.

It is important to remember, when asking the horse for collection, not to restrict the horse's head and neck and force them into a tight position. The head and neck must be relaxed, as must the rest of the frame of the horse – particularly the top line. If the head and neck are forced into a position that restricts them the rest of the body will be restricted and therefore tense. The horse must be prepared to shorten his outline because you have asked him to, not because you have forced him. There must be a relaxation of every part of his body even in those powerful hind legs coming under him.

If you compare the outlines of a horse in extension with a horse in collection you will see a significant difference in the length of the body and fig. 102 illustrates this.

When collection has progressed, the horse should start to lower his quarters as he shifts the weight, carrying even more from the front legs to the hind legs. Now you are really going places and you will feel a huge difference in the lightness and elevation of his gait.

Collection is physically demanding for the horse and does tend to make him tense his muscles when he is in this

Fig. 102 Collection and extension.
(Top) Horse in extension.
(Bottom) Horse in collection.

compressed shape for any length of time. We want the work of the horse to be as free moving and relaxed as possible at all times, and therefore it is not good to do too much collected work. It is also a good idea to do alternate collected work with free moving relaxed work. Something such as lengthened strides or round and down will help the horse stretch his frame.

The ultimate in collection is 'piaffe', where the horse actually trots on the spot without moving forwards. The 'passage' is not quite as collected as the piaffe but the elevation is greater. In passage the horse uses a great deal of energy with a very small amount of forward movement. It is one of the most beautiful movements to watch being performed.

Working through
This is when the horse works forward from your leg in an energetic and responsive manner and allows that forward energy to be harnessed by the reins. It is the ultimate that you will be seeking when schooling your horse. The horse is willingly giving an energetic forward going movement and at the same time happily submitting to the control of your hands. It can only be achieved when the horse is physically supple and able to round its top line in the correct shape.

If the horse is coming through properly, his frame has been stretched, his back and hocks are coming under him and he is able to lower his quarters. He is able to accept the driving power of the rider's legs into the contact of the bridle. As gradually more power is developed behind he is able to accept this power without fighting the control of the bit but by allowing his body to alter its shape and become more compact. He is now able, to a greater or lesser extent, to lower his quarters and take a greater proportion of his weight on his hind legs.

If your horse is coming through properly, the energy and forward movement that you are able to generate when the horse is travelling in a straight line should be maintained when you ask for a more difficult movement such as shoulder in or a smallish circle.

8

The Nature of Horses

If you understand the nature and behaviour of horses you will get the best out of them both as friends and as athletes. If you know what they do in certain circumstances, and why they do it, training them is much easier and more successful. Because you understand them better, you will develop a closer relationship and you will both enjoy each other's company more!

Much of the horse's behaviour is innate. It is inborn, instinctive behaviour, derived from their existence when living in the wild. They developed this over thousands of years in order to survive in a harsh, cruel environment. Though they have been domesticated for a long time, this instinctive behaviour has not left them. We must strive to understand it, because it forms as much a part of them as their desire to eat and to sleep. We need to research and examine it closely, because it forms the pegs upon which we will hang the development of their training. It is not possible to go against the nature of the horse. We have to accept, understand and work with them as they are.

To train horses as efficiently and effectively as possible, we must understand how they learn, and, based on this, use the best methods to teach them.

Humans are often guilty of anthropomorphism – we like to give our animals the characters of humans. We must take care not to fall into the trap of always believing they think and behave as we do. We must maintain an awareness of their true nature. However, there are certain ways in which humans and horses are similar; for example in their need for companionship, their social order and their body language. It is largely because of these similarities that humans and horses get on so well with each other.

Peaceful, sociable survival

Horses are by nature gentle creatures – they eat grass and they do not kill other animals. They do not normally need aggression to survive. If threatened they will flee and because they are so fast they will outrun most of their predators.

The main aim in the lives of horses is to survive both as individuals and as a breed. To survive as a breed they need to mate and reproduce. To survive as an individual they need to be able to find food, and recognise their predators; to see or hear them coming and to run away. This is why they are social animals. It is essential to their survival. All members of the herd are on the lookout for threatening situations. Because there are many horses in the herd, each looking in a different direction while they graze, they have a better chance of seeing, hearing or smelling a potential threat than a lone animal would have. Being in a group also deters a potential predator who might consider taking on a vulnerable lone animal, but not a group. A lone horse would not survive for long in the wild and he knows it. A predator may attack and kill him if he lacks the protection of the herd. If he was part of a group, a predator would know that the combined forces of the herd would easily fight him off, and possibly injure him. So he keeps away.

So a horse has a strong instinct to belong to a group. To be isolated could mean death. Because of this, all horses crave company. It is this instinct – to have company and be part of a group – which holds the group together and forms the basis of their social structure. Horses within a group frequently reinforce this social structure by mutual grooming. They first touch noses and, provided there has been no objection from either of them, they will go on to groom each other on their manes, withers and sometimes croup. They are effectively saying that they are friends, and that they will look out for each other. This process initiates or reinforces their relationship, which makes them care about each other and want to stick together as a group. It is often described as bonding. They are rather like the members of a large family, all loving each other and looking out for each other (though not necessarily liking each other!). They will also pair off and form lasting friendships with particular horses. This will often be with horses of a similar age and maybe the same sex. They are not unlike humans in this way. During the ritual of mutual grooming, the heartbeat of both horses will drop as they become more relaxed. Horses will eventually mutually groom with all the members of their group, thus reinforcing the bond between the whole group. They will mutually groom with the rest of the group much less often than with their specific friends. These friendships are very important to horses, and they will display a strong desire to be reunited with their "friend", if they are separated, by calling loudly and by showing agitation.

When horses initiate or re-establish their relationship they often touch noses. The horse's mouth and nose are very responsive to touch and smell. They are the most sensitive parts of the animal, with many, many nerve endings capable of sending to their brain detailed messages about the surface and smell of what they are investigating. This helps them perform delicate tasks with their mouth, such as selecting the best grass from amongst the weeds.

The nose and mouth are the first parts of another horse's anatomy that a horse will allow into his personal space, before checking him out and letting him further in. The horse uses his outstretched nose and mouth to sense what the other animal is – keeping him at his distance until he is sure. This gesture roughly compares to the human hand-shake – they are touching, and giving out messages of civility and friendship, but in fact still weighing one another up. The nose and mouth are also areas used by horses to give reassurance (and perhaps affection) to another horse, as with a mare touching her foal. The next stage would be when the horse lets the other horse further into his space, and they mutually groom each other. Now they are two best mates with their arms round one another.

Because it is such an important part of horses' survival, they are programmed to have a strong need for familiar equine company. If deprived of the company of other horses, they will soon make similar lasting friendships with other animals, including humans. Their strong need for company eventually overcomes the desire for the specific company of a horse, and they will make do with just about anyone. Their instinct tells them that to survive they must have company even if it is not equine.

Recognition

The ability to recognise others is essential if this social system is to work. There is no doubt that horses show a marked ability to recognise other horses by using their visual, auditory and olfactory (smell) senses, all of which are well developed.

Domination

Within the group, horses will develop a pecking order. A hierarchy evolves. Each horse knows where he stands in relation to all the other horses in the group in different circumstances. This dominance is based on the threat of violence from the dominant horse, and on the subservient animal's fear of it. (In the lower orders of human life this still occurs, but in more civilised society the violence or threat of violence has been replaced by outward manifestations of superiority, such as a cultured voice or an expensive car.) Once the domination is established between horses, it is actually a way of avoiding violence. Each animal knows his place in the hierarchy, and will respect the dominance of other animals in order to avoid being hurt. Simply placing his ears back will often be enough for a dominant horse to remind another of his subservience. Occasionally the domination of one animal by another may be challenged, particularly as the younger horses mature and the older ones become weaker. Presumably the normally subservient horse always has his eyes open for a chink in the armour of the dominating horse, though, as with humans, some horses are happier in the lower part of the pecking order. Life is often easier there!

At times this hierarchy can be upset by bonding. A horse from lower down in the rankings may bond with a horse who is dominant. While those two horses are together, the lower ranking horse will take on the protection of the higher-ranking one, and gain respect from those who would normally dominate him. Because of this, it pays a horse to bond with those who are dominant. He gains from the strength and protection of this higher-ranking companion. Horses, rather like humans, will choose a powerful dominant friend if they have the chance. This is why it pays humans to be strong, powerful and dominant with their horses. Their strength makes the prospect of bonding with them more attractive to the horse.

Violence and the horse
Discipline and social order are an essential feature in the life of horses, but the horse rarely wishes to be violent for the sake of violence. He uses the threat of it to maintain his domination and gain the benefits of his superiority, such as to be the first to get to the hay or whatever. If, however, his threat is ignored, he will resort to violence to maintain his position or to control the situation. For example a horse will often kick out at another horse, even his own "friends" or offspring, if they overstep the mark or invade his space without permission. In the same way a mare will sometimes bite her own foal if he misbehaves or annoys her.

Matriarchal mare
Because horses are such social animals, they need a social code within the group so that they can peacefully coexist. The hierarchical system combined with the social system achieves this for most of the time, but beyond this there is a need for group leaders, or a "policeman" of the social code. This is often a matriarchal mare. She is the schoolmistress of the outfit, responsible for organising the horses in the group. She sometimes uses aggression to dominate its unruly members. As spotted by Monty Roberts, the original "horse whisperer", in extreme cases she uses isolation as a punishment and pushes out a trouble maker,

keeping him away from the group and isolating him from their protection. He, knowing this to be a threat of death, will eventually signal to her that he will behave and she will let him back into the herd.

Stallion

The stallion's main function is to get the mares of his group pregnant. He also uses his superior strength, where necessary, to fight off both equine rivals and non-equine aggressors. He is responsible for maintaining the quality of the offspring of the group by making sure he (the best) is the father of them. Nature puts upon him the responsibility of keeping away and, if necessary, fighting off other stallions, to stop the possibility of his mares producing offspring from an inferior mate.

Flight animals

Horses are flight animals – their first reaction is to run away from things that frighten them. If they hear or see something they are unfamiliar with, instead of investigating it, they run away and ask questions later. If they feel pain they almost always instinctively run, rather than fighting the source of the pain.

Memory

Horses have exceptional memories – like elephants, they never forget. In the wild they use their memories to relocate to watering holes and good grazing. They also need to remember, and recognise, their mates and companions. They never seem to forget a lesson, once it is learnt, nor a face, a place or a bad experience.

Communication

Horses have limited vocal language, extending only to the whinny, the nicker, the hard blow and the squeal. Because they are such social animals they need to communicate with each other to a greater degree than this limited vocal language will allow. So, they have evolved a means of communication with their bodies and their faces. Sometimes this body language is very readable, such as when a horse bares his teeth, or turns his quarters in the direction of his victim. Sometimes it is very subtle, as when a horse lowers his head to avoid confrontation. Because this subject is so important and so complex I have devoted a separate chapter to it (Chapter 11).

Smell

Horses have a sense of smell that is vastly better than our own. They can tell who passed by quite a long time ago. If the wind is in the right direction, they may be able to tell where that animal is, even at quite a distance away. If a (forgive the pun) passing horse leaves droppings on the ground, another horse of his acquaintance could identify him from these droppings, even if they have been overlaid by other droppings. Horses recognise the smell of other horses and other animals on our clothes, or even the smell of familiar places.

Frequent exposure

When horses are repeatedly subjected to something which they would normally find frightening, but which doesn't harm them, they learn to ignore it. For example, if they heard a loud noise in the field beside them, horses grazing would undoubtedly run away from it. If this noise happened again, they would probably still run away. Suppose the noise was repeated day after day, and the horses had not been harmed in any way. After about a week the horses would cease to run away, and possibly even to acknowledge it. They have learnt that, because the noise didn't cause them any harm, it was not worth wasting energy running away from it. A typical example is where a horse is put into a field with a railway line beside it. At first the horse is startled by the sight and sound of a train. After a few days he will not even lift his head when a train passes by. It is important that the noise (or whatever) is repeated many times during a short period. If it had happened as many times but over a longer period they would not become as accustomed to it. For example, if a loud noise had been repeated once a month, for six or seven months, the horses would probably still run away from it each time they heard it.

How do horses learn?

Horses are very clever at associating related events. They learn what to expect in certain situations, and, therefore, how to react. Imagine that a horse heard a dog growling, followed by the appearance of a dog who then rushed out and bit him. The horse will remember that, every time he hears a dog growling, he should move out of the way first, just in case the dog bites him.

A dominant member of the herd might flatten his ears when another horse came too near. If the less dominant herd member hadn't been aware of the meaning of this signal, and didn't move out of the way, he would probably end up being kicked. He would learn by association that, when a horse puts his ears back, it means keep out of the way. In other words the horse learns that, when one thing happens, it is often followed by another related occurrence. If the horse learns that things which no longer used to be a danger now are, he may save his life by learning to run away from the new threat. Similarly, if he learns that a thing which used to be a threat no longer is, he will save valuable energy by not running away from it any more.

In their search for good food or water, horses will remember their location by associating features of the landscape with the food or water. One of the purposes of learning is survival. A horse's ability to learn from experience has helped him to survive as a breed, and we can use it in our efforts to train him.

Vision

A horse's vision is different from ours – he can see almost 360 degrees around him. He is blind only in about three degrees immediately behind his head. Because his eyes are situated on the sides of his head he is also unable to see in a tiny wedge right in front of his nose. The right eye will see virtually all that is immediately in front of the horse, including approximately 32 degrees to the left of the horse's nose. It will also see to the side of him, and behind him to where the rider is sitting, but will see this with only one eye. The left eye will see the same on the left side. Apart from the small blind spot in front of his nose, the 65

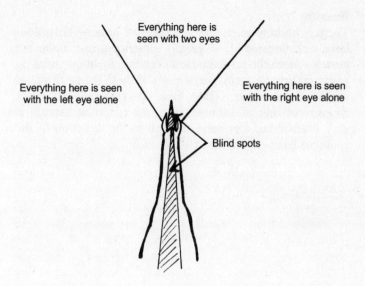

Fig. 103 The vision of the horse.

degrees in front of the horse is seen with both eyes (binocular vision) and hence virtually everything within this area is seen clearly. Apart from the blind spot behind the horse all else is seen with only one eye, either the right or the left, which is obviously not as good as vision with two eyes. Using this monocular method, the horse has peripheral sight that allows him to see almost immediately behind him. But the further to the back of him that he looks, the more the image becomes blurred. Something that is behind him looks distorted. It is therefore more likely to give a horse a fright than something closer to the front, where he would be able to make it out clearly. If the horse is unable to identify it, he will presume it is dangerous and shy away to a position where he can see it better.

A horse's vision is not as good as ours in daylight, but, due to the construction of his eye, he is better able to make use of the limited light available at night. Hence his night vision is better than ours.

Hearing

There is nothing to suggest that horses' hearing is particularly well developed, or greatly superior to our own, but horses definitely rely on their hearing to know what is going on around them, particularly if there is any threat of approaching danger. Their ears are especially flexible. Because of this, and the shape of the ear, their hearing is very directional. The ears can turn to the direction of the sound to hear it even better.

9

Working with the Horse's Nature

The knowledge we have acquired about horses now needs applying to our relationship with them.

Keeping close to nature
In his natural environment the horse moves around with a group of other horses. He spends his entire day eating, resting and sleeping in the outdoors. In this outdoor life he wanders freely and constantly has the companionship of other horses.

We use horses for our benefit, not for theirs, so to suit our needs we change their environment. Instead of being out at grass all day, some horses spend part or all of their lives in a stable, eating dried grass and concentrated food. The better quality food makes them able to perform better, and the reduced eating time makes them more available for work. To a greater or lesser degree it is inevitable that we make our horses live in an unnatural environment. But, the more we interfere with their natural lifestyle, the more risk we run of psychological damage manifesting itself in bad habits, vices, tension etc. If we can keep their living conditions as close to nature as possible, the horse should have a more balanced personality.

Some owners hardly let the horse out of the stable except to work. This is to reserve his energy and enthusiasm for work, and to stop him from hurting himself when running around in the field. If these horses were allowed to run round in a field every day for at least an hour or two, they arguably might end up being happier, working harder and performing better. Nevertheless there are some horses who take to permanent life in a stable like a duck to water, strongly resisting the potential hazards of the elements when offered them – particularly if it is raining!

It isn't always possible, but if we can also provide our horses with company in their field, preferably equine, they will be much happier. It is the natural lifestyle of the species, and the one in which they will be most relaxed. Again, some horses prove the exception to the rule and prefer life on their own, particularly if they have the constant attention of an adoring owner.

One cruel tradition that exists is to wean foals from their mothers by locking them in a stable for days on end without any company whatsoever. The foals are terrified and desperately lonely. It is so unnecessary. If the foal has other company in the field that he is used to, and happy with, he will settle very well with this company if his mother is taken away. It can be made even less of a shock to the foal if his mother has previously been taken away from him for short periods, so that he has had a chance to experience life without her before the extended separation at weaning.

Using the horse's social code

There is something very special about the way in which horses relate to each other. Their system of discipline and social order makes it easy for us to dominate them in order to train them. Their ability to learn from associations and repeated exposure makes them good pupils. Their social code is tailor-made for us to step in and become part of it.

The importance of this social conditioning is borne out by the subsequent behaviour of foals who are hand reared by humans. They frequently grow up very difficult to handle. It is as if they think of themselves as human, not horse, and expect to play life by our rules. They haven't learnt the socialising skills of horses which are fundamental to our ability to school them. In view of this, one might wonder just how important it is for us to handle young

212

horses, particularly foals? Is it possible we may be interfering in the socialising process which is taught by other horses at this time? Should we leave nature to take its course and reap the benefits later, or do young horses benefit from being handled by humans frequently? I suspect that it *is* more beneficial to handle young stock, provided it is handled with proper respect for the discipline and social order of the species. If, in your handling of a young horse, you do not reinforce the discipline of the herd, you may well be teaching it a bad lesson for life. If you let a foal think that a human is normally dominated by the horse, it may be difficult to reverse this belief later.

The main aim in horses' lives has not changed with domesticity. They still have a strong drive to survive both as a species and individually – just like all animals. Obviously their sexual drive has survived intact, which is why we geld young male horses who are not needed for breeding. We fear that their attention may be diverted to sexual matters when they should be working for us.

Their instincts tell them that to survive as an individual they have to find food, water and companionship. Their life, domesticated by humans, normally gives them all of these.

Social organisation

The desire of horses to have company, and bond with their companions, still exists in domestication. Because we are their close companions, they can and will bond with us just as they bond with their equine companions. Part of the bonding process that horses go through is their grooming of each other around the neck and wither. When you groom your horse you are not only cleaning him; you are nurturing the relationship between you. Horses groom each other in the specified area which they "allow" the other horse into. When we groom, we go beyond the frontiers of this area, grooming all over the body. Often horses resent this. By making them accept it, we are both establishing and/or re-establishing our mutual trust and also our domination of them. This also applies when we stroke our horses.

If we are brave enough to confront horses and dominate

them, this makes us a more desirable friend. They know that we will also be strong enough and brave enough to protect them. While we maintain this domination and strength, their desire to keep us a friend will remain. Add this to the closeness that is achieved by bonding with our horses, and we have the perfect combination to have a happy, compliant horse.

The nose and the mouth of the horse have something in common with the hands of humans. If we are meeting a new horse, or saying hello to our horse in the morning, placing our hand on his nose is seen by him as a greeting. We want him to let us happily into his personal space and accept us as his friend. We are merely aping nature and making him feel as comfortable as possible in our company. The next stage in the greeting is to groom our horse, particularly around the withers and neck. We know his heartbeat will become lower and he should become even more relaxed in our company. Just as horses strengthen their relationship by grooming each other, we can also strengthen our relationship with horses by grooming and stroking them.

Domination, the hierarchical system and seeking a strong friend through bonding

Horses would rather bond with another horse who is well up in the pecking order; a strong, dominant horse. He will share his social status when he is with him, and he will have his protection if threatened. Through bonding with horses we can achieve the closeness to them that they would normally reserve for other horses. Perhaps even more so, because we supply their food, and also because of the role we take on – that of a dominant trainer. If we can replace the dominant horse by being a dominant, strong trainer, our horse will be happy to have our company. We can become his special friend, whom he will want to obey because he wants to retain our protective friendship.

A horse will seek our company because of the strength we manifest in dominating him. Like a child he will feel safer with us. The stronger we are with him – the more decisions we make for him, the more relaxed he will be. He feels we will look after him and is less nervous about having to look out for himself.

Nonetheless, a horse will often test your strength if he sees you manifesting some weakness. He may put in a challenge to your supremacy. There are two reasons for this. Perhaps the horse is naturally dominant and wishes to be your boss. If this is the case you may well have something of a fight on your hands, as he may resort to violence to establish his dominance. Whatever he does, you must be prepared to prove to him that he is wrong and that you are the braver. Horses are great users of bluff to gain a better social position. Humans can employ a similar subterfuge. Try to convince him that you are the dominant one by the body language you use. Occasionally, sadly, it may be necessary to use some physical punishment as proof if your bluff is called.

It could be that your behaviour is the reason for the challenge. If you show weakness your horse may try to achieve supremacy. Perhaps you have flinched if he has turned his quarters towards you, and he has sensed your nervousness. He may wish himself to be on that higher plane, or he may be testing you to see if you still possess the ability to dominate him. If you are able to maintain your domination, the horse may be quite happy to see that you have lost none of your strength and are still capable of looking after him. It is similar to the situation that arises when an insecure child tests the strength of his parent. When the child behaves badly it is often because of insecurity. The child is worried that the parents are not strong and are unable to cope with and protect him. The child actually wants to be disciplined because he wants evidence that his parents are strong. A horse's challenge to authority is often based on a very similar psychology – he doesn't actually want to get away with it, and wants to know that his dominator is still strong enough to look after him. Horses are great users of and believers in bluff, in the wild. In the domestic situation most handlers use bluff to keep their horses believing they are stronger and fiercer than their horses.

One of the most useful equine traits for the purpose of

schooling is the horse's instinctive reliance on the hierarchical system. He subjugates his will to the will of the dominant horse. We can replace the dominant horse in this relationship and become the boss. We must instil some fear in the horse, that we are capable of violence if he does not do as we wish. We do not actually have to hurt the horse to do this, because horses are so skilful in interpreting our body language. We adapt their body language, which fortunately is often similar to our own, to tell them we are superior. For example, if you were confident of your ability to handle the horse, you would walk confidently into the stable, with your head up and maintaining eye contact with the horse. You would not be nervous or hesitant when handling him (see Chapter 11). Horses recognise this behaviour as that of a dominant personality and most horses accept the domination without challenge. Whether he challenges or not largely depends on his natural bravery and confidence. If he does, you must be ready with an immediate confirmation of the threat you have previously been bluffing about. If, for example, a horse kicked you or bit you, or threatened to do either of these things, not only is it forgivable to smack him firmly, it is essential. You must deal with him as another horse would deal with him. He does not understand anything else. You must remain his boss otherwise he will become yours and you will be at his mercy. Horses who are allowed to become the boss can become dangerous, and are always difficult to school.

Violence

Horses use violence or the threat of violence to establish their status among other horses. When horses meet for the first time, they must find out which will be dominant. If one horse thinks of himself as the boss, he probably employs all the means at his disposal to convince the other horse that he is the strongest and most courageous. He probably stands as tall as he can, with his head and neck elevated, so that he looks as big as possible. If this is enough to keep the other horse at a distance, it may be all that he needs to do to convince the other horse of his superiority and there will be no violence. If the other horse also fancies his chances of being the boss, he also draws himself up to his full height, and the two horses probably approach each other. A squealing contest could then ensue, which may settle the matter, with the horse having the bravest, loudest squeal accepted as dominant. If this doesn't achieve a clear leader the two may well fight. After one or all of these stages has been gone through, superiority becomes established, and they should resort to a peaceful coexistence.

Because of this possibility of fighting between newly introduced horses, one has to be vigilant when putting a new horse into a field with another horse or horses. If there is ever going to be a fight between them, it will be in the first day or two. After they have established who is to be the boss, they usually settle down and get on with each other very well. During these first few days you need to keep a careful eye on them. If you see the telltale signs of fighting, without putting yourself at risk, attempt to separate them. If possible, allow horses to meet for the first time over a fence, or preferably a hedge, so that they can decide on their ranking without hurting each other and without giving their owners heart attacks!

Flight animals
Horses normally run away from pain or a threat of it. They do not normally confront the source of the pain. By and large this makes them easier to train, although sometimes this instinct to flee can make them behave oddly. One such circumstance is when the bit is hurting the horse's mouth. When the rider asks the horse to slow or stop, if the bit hurts, the horse may well run faster rather than slowing. Inevitably the rider will take a stronger hold on the bit, and the horse will run all the faster. He is running away from the pain and doesn't realise that he is making it worse for himself.

A horse will also run away from pain caused by an ill-fitting saddle.

Both of these situations could cause the horse to become out of the rider's control and hence very dangerous.

Memory

We must always remain aware of the superb memory of the horse. If he has suffered in particular circumstances, he will remember the suffering and the cause of it. It is very important to make learning experiences good experiences. When he does as we wish, we should make him feel good with a reward, like stopping work. We must also avoid bad experiences. If he is punished unfairly during schooling (particularly if he is a she) he will associate the punishment with what you are trying to teach him. It will probably mar this type of work for a very long time.

If we can give the horse good memories to associate with our training and handling, these will also stay for a long time. Good associations should be made with everything you do with your horse, if you want to make life easy and pleasant for both of you. Tacking up and grooming can be contrived to be good (or bad) experiences as can boxing, injecting and shoeing. It all depends on the way you handle him at these times and the pleasure that you can add to potentially unpleasant occasions. If he misbehaves because he is frightened or in pain, and you get cross with him or hit him, you will make this behaviour even worse the next time. From thinking there might be something to be afraid of when, for example, you put the saddle on, now he is certain there is something to fear, because you added to and confirmed his fear by hurting him.

Horses' memory can be employed to advantage in other ways. Maybe we wish to teach an exercise, particularly, perhaps, a transition. If we ask the horse to do this at the same place in the arena each time, he will learn to expect it when he arrives there. This, however, can be both an advantage and a disadvantage. It can make the lesson easier to teach, but it can make the horse presume we want to perform at that point, whether or not we have actually asked him to. In other words he learns to anticipate our commands. After he has learnt the command, you should then ask him to perform it in different places, and insist that he doesn't make the transition without your requesting it.

Frequent exposure

We have already come across the situation where a horse is frequently exposed to something that would normally be frightening, but never followed up with any pain or suffering. Eventually the horse will come to ignore it. This has obvious potential advantages. If the horse is frightened of traffic, then, from a safe distance, let him see a lot of it. Soon he will accept traffic as normal and non-threatening. If a horse is nervous when he goes to a show, take him to lots of shows until he realises there is nothing to worry about. He will soon learn to relax. If he hates water, make him go into it a lot. He will soon learn there is nothing to fear from monsters of the deep. Police horses are repeatedly exposed to crowds and loud noises, unruly behaviour and fire until they learn not to be frightened of them because they have not hurt them.

This exposure must be repeated many times during a relatively short period if the horse is to learn to ignore it. For example, if you want your horse to become accustomed to shows, you need to take him to a show every weekend for, say, five or six weeks. When he has become accustomed to it, there is no need to visit shows regularly as he has learnt that there is nothing to fear there. The same would be true of water. It would be of no use whatsoever forcing your horse through water just before a cross-country competition. He will remember the force but forget that there was nothing frightening in the water. If you took him through water virtually every day, preferably at different places for five or six days he would realise AND remember there was nothing in water that hurts him. Remember also to avoid punishment when trying to get him into water. He would remember the pain and associate it with the water, and that would make him even more frightened of water.

The same applies to many things that horses do not like doing. For example going into and travelling in a horsebox or trailer. Get them in using the least possible force – take your time – reward them. When they are in, give them the best journey possible and make it short if you can. Just go round the block the first time, and very slowly. If they arrive back home after 10 minutes and it hasn't been too bad an experience for them, and if they do this again several times, they will learn and remember that travelling need hold no fears for them.

There are times, however, when this disregard of frequent exposure is counter-productive. For example, when a horse is not forward going, sometimes riders get into the habit of constantly kicking, or flapping, their legs on the horse's sides. Initially the horse knows that to feel those legs on his sides means he must go faster. However, he becomes so used to feeling them, without anything unpleasant happening to him, that he learns to ignore them. You end up with a horse who has become unresponsive to the pressure of the legs on his side.

Learning by association

Horses are adept at learning by making associations. In their natural existence they use this for survival. For example, when they learn what is dangerous and to keep clear of it: the black dog has tried to bite him so in future he keeps away from it. He will learn this lesson very quickly. Learning by association teaches horses to respect the social order in the herd. If there is a horse that often kicks out when another horse goes behind it, the other horse will learn to respect this horse and not go too close to its back legs.

Associations also help horses to remember where to find food and water. At home this is easily learnt, but in the wild, when travelling each day over territory that hasn't been seen for several weeks or months, developing an ability to associate food and water with particular features in the landscape is more than useful. It also demonstrates how good is their memory of the lessons learnt this way. This ability to learn by association is essential to their survival and is therefore an integral part of their nature.

In domesticity we can use their adeptness at learning by association to help us in our training programme. We can use it, together with negative and positive reinforcement (see page 223), to teach them virtually everything they need to know. They learn to accept our domination through associating unpleasant results from bad behaviour, and pleasant consequences with good behaviour. They learn many of the aids through association. If you want them to slow down, you increase the contact on the reins. When they slow, the contact is reduced. When these aids are repeated several times, they learn that, if they slow up, the contact on the reins is reduced, which they find more pleasant than increased contact. This is negative reinforcement. At the same time they learn to associate the increased pressure of the bit with a request to slow down. As you gradually reduce the strength of this aid to merely closing the hands, they still associate this with being asked to slow down. The same principle is used in applying the legs to get them to go on. At first the horse may obey the aids because of a physical reason, but soon he learns to do as you ask because of the associations. Because of this you are able to reduce the strength of the command. A request to move off or go faster may well start off as a strong leg aid. You can gradually reduce it until eventually it becomes a discreet squeeze with the legs as the horse learns what is required. The same concepts apply to the other aids.

There are times when the horse obeys commands which we do not realise we are giving. Have you ever been about to ask your horse to canter or trot, when he does so before you have actually asked him? You have done nothing – did you think he was a mind reader? Well, you may have *thought* you did nothing. But when most riders are about to ask for a transition, particularly an upwards one, they invariably shorten the rein and sit up more. They then give the horse the aid to make the transition. After a time, the horse grows to associate the sitting up and the shortening of the rein with a request for trot or canter. He knows you are about to ask for it – so he obliges and does it. He is not being naughty. In fact, in his mind he is being good, so you should never blame him. It is you who are at fault for changing your position before you ask for the transition. This is one reason why it is important to keep your position unchanged until you actually give the aid.

Hearing

Horses rely fairly heavily on their sense of hearing to warn them of approaching danger. If anything impedes the horse's hearing he will be nervous, worrying all the time in case there is some danger that he is unable to hear. One such problem is when the wind is blowing noisily. It is impossible for a horse to hear well in these conditions. He is naturally nervous and spooky, trying to turn his head this way and that to see better what is happening around him, and overreacting to any noises or movement he might be able to hear or see.

It is interesting to note the directional hearing of horses. You will have noticed their ears move around a lot, sometimes facing front or to the side or the back. When they turn their ears like this they are listening in the direction of the open part of their ears. If you are riding, ideally you want to see his ears turning backwards towards you. This means he is listening to you and concentrating on what you are doing and asking him to do. If his ears are moving all over the place, or are turned away, you know you do not have his full attention. Wherever his ears are pointing, that is where his attention is.

The direction of the horse's ears sometimes tells us where he is looking. He can see around the back of him, so he doesn't always have to turn his head to look at something. If it suits him to keep his head facing front (for example if he is eating), he can still see, albeit less clearly, something to the side. He can turn an ear better to listen to any noise coming from that direction. If his head is straight on, but his ear is facing sideways, he is almost certainly giving his attention to whatever his ear is pointing at. Research has shown that, in the human brain, the auditory and visual parts are activated at the same time. It would appear that, in the horse, there is also a relationship between hearing and seeing. Rather like people who wear glasses and say they hear better when they are wearing them.

10

How Do We Teach Horses?

There are five main ways in which horses learn and in which we teach them. These are: positive reinforcement, negative reinforcement, punishment, frequent exposure and learning by association.

● **Positive reinforcement** is when we reward the horse for doing as we ask. For example if we ride our horse at a jump and he jumps it we could give him a reward such as a carrot, a pat or stopping work. Thus he learns that, if he does as he is told, he is rewarded. When he jumps it is pleasant for him because he gets a reward – he is learning to associate the jump with pleasure.

If, at the same time as giving him the carrot, you pat him and talk softly to him, he associates the pat and the voice with the reward. After a while the pat and the voice become a reward in themselves – this is secondary positive reinforcement.

● **Negative reinforcement** is when the horse feels unpleasant sensations which go away when he does as you want. When you want the horse to stop or slow, you increase the contact and therefore the pressure on the horse's mouth. When he slows or stops, the pressure goes away. The horse has learnt that if he feels pressure on his mouth, and he slows or stops, that pressure will go away. It is *very* important for the rider to know that the contact must be reduced when the horse does as he is told, otherwise the horse would become confused. The same is true of leg aids, whether they be given to drive the horse forwards or sideways. When the horse does as required, the increase of the leg aids must cease, so that the horse knows he has done what was wanted.

● **Punishment** is when the horse is subjected to an unpleasant sensation for doing what is wrong. This punishment is normally physical, i.e. pain, such as a smack from a whip, or by making the horse work hard, but it can come to be verbal. If, at the same time as hitting the horse, you shout at him he will come to associate the verbal admonishment with the pain. Before long he feels as punished by the raised voice as he was by the whip.

● **Frequent exposure** (as discussed in Chapter 9). We use this method to accustom our horses to something which they might otherwise find frightening. By seeing it or experiencing it frequently without any harm to themselves they learn not to fear it.

● **Learning by association** (as discussed in Chapter 9). We use this principle in many ways. Every time you put your legs on the sides of the horse, he associates it with going forwards. Suppose that at the same time you clicked your tongue. He would learn by association that, every time you either clicked your tongue or put your legs on his side, he should go forwards. The same would be true when the horse learns to stop, or go more slowly, because he feels pressure on the bit. He associates pressure on the bit with going more slowly. Originally he learnt this, and to move away from the leg, through negative reinforcement. As you can see, there can be more than one type of learning taking place at the same time.

Teaching new things
It is important to understand the learning process properly if you are intending to teach something new. When the horse was first ridden he knew absolutely nothing. Not that when the leg is put on he had to go forward, nor that when

he felt more pressure from the bit in his mouth he had to stop or slow. He didn't even know that feeling pressure from the bit on one side of his mouth meant turn right or left. All these things had to be taught to him, slowly and painstakingly, little by little. Eventually the horse learned to associate the leg and rein aids with what the rider wanted.

When you ask your horse to do something that he has not done before, he probably won't understand what you want. Be prepared to show him, in as clear a way as possible, what you require of him. Do not presume that, because you use the correct aids for a new manoeuvre or exercise, he will automatically comprehend what you want him to do. Everything has to be taught to him. He is not psychic. If someone hasn't already shown him what is required, you will have to. You will have to devise a method of teaching him, based on the above and incorporating the correct aids. You will have to be patient – at first he won't have a clue about what you want him to do. Your aids will have to be clear, and a little stronger than normal, so that there is no confusion for him. They must always be consistent, so that he learns to associate your aids with what you want him to do. The exercise must be repeated until he has thoroughly learnt his lesson.

Errors in behaviour management
Sometimes we inadvertently teach our horse to behave badly. For example, a horse tied up and left alone is often unhappy. He may therefore paw the ground or make a noise. His concerned owner comes to him to make sure that there is nothing wrong with him, or even to scold him for his behaviour. The horse quickly realises that, whenever he paws the ground, someone will come to him. Because he prefers to have someone with him, he continues pawing the ground or making a noise. He wants to keep someone coming to see him even if that person is cross with him. To a horse this is better than being alone. The moral of this story is: do not go and see him when he does this (unless you really do think he is putting himself in danger).

Be careful with punishment as a training method. You

must be sure that the horse has been naughty rather than confused. Punishment must be administered immediately after the wrongdoing. The horse must know that the punishment is the consequence of his behaviour. If there is a delay, and for this reason or any other reason, the horse is unsure why he is being punished, it will produce confusion, and probably even worse behaviour.

It is also important that the horse does not associate his punishment with the work he is doing. If, for example, he refused several jumps and was smacked for each refusal, he would probably associate being smacked with jumping. He may always hate jumping as a result. If the horse is difficult about jumping, it is essential to find another way that is not unpleasant. Perhaps you could start with smaller jumps, praising and rewarding him every time he jumped. This would replace punishment with reward or positive reinforcement, always a step in the right direction!

11

How Do Horses Communicate?

I think it must be almost every horse owner's dream to have a horse that could talk, one's own "Mr. Ed", for those of us old enough to remember T.V.'s talking horse! What most of don't realise is that horses do talk to us in many ways. They have a very varied system of communication, based largely on body language, which can help us understand what they are trying to communicate. If we can learn this language we can communicate with them by the same system. Good communication leads to a better understanding of each other's needs, and an improved relationship with them.

Because horses are such social beings, communication between themselves and other members of their group is very important to them. It is a vital factor in organising and maintaining the social cohesion which is essential for their survival.

How do horses communicate with each other?

By sound

The nicker. This is a low, soft sound that is usually associated with pleasure, either experienced or anticipated by the horse. A mare would nicker on being reunited with her foal, as would the hungry horse when his owner appears bearing food, or the lonely horse when company approaches. The horse is saying, "This is good, I'm happy".

The whinny. This is used to tell other horses where the whinnying horse is, and asks them to respond by whinnying so that their location can be judged. It means, "I'm here – where are you?". It is high pitched and travels well over distance. Horses are skilled at judging the direction from which the sound has come. When grazing, horses normally keep other members of their group in sight. They, therefore, tend to rely more on visual signals than on sound. When horses are out of sight of each other, audible signals replace visual ones. This is why stabled horses often call if they are unable to see each other. It is not necessarily a sound of distress, often only a communication. You can tell from the pitch of the whinny when it becomes a sound of distress. It becomes higher and louder. Some horses are particularly unhappy if they are on their own. If they are able to communicate with another horse, but unable to be with him, they will become even more distressed.

The hard blow or snort. This is a sound produced when there is something that is potentially frightening or interesting about. The animal who has made it often turns and stares at whatever has caught his attention before, during and after he makes the sound. It is a loud noise and commands the attention of the other horses. The snorting horse is almost saying, "Have you seen this? I don't like the look of it – be careful".

The squeal. This sound is often made when two horses meet. They approach, cautiously touch noses and one or the other of them may squeal, or perhaps both of them squeal. When they touch noses they are weighing each other up. The squeal is a challenge to the other horse. The squealing horse is saying he is the boss. It is often enough to establish him as the dominant horse, provided that the other horse accepts this situation. If the other horse doesn't respond to the challenge, he will not squeal. This means he accepts the first horse as the dominant one.

If the second horse does squeal, it means he is not happy to accept the first horse as his superior. At this stage the horse with the loudest squeal may win the contest. In the animal kingdom, he who can make the loudest noise is often the largest and most dangerous, and therefore the one to be respected. A little bit like two small boys in the playground, trying to face each other off before a fight. Their voices will gradually rise until they are shouting, because the volume of the voice makes promise of a stronger person. In the same way, the horse making the larger noise asserts that he is stronger. If this is not sufficient to settle the matter, the conversation may turn into a fight between the two horses. Neither admits to being the lesser, and physical strength will have to win the day. Not all horses meeting in this way squeal. Sometimes they merely introduce themselves to each other and are happy with each other's existing status. They walk away without making a sound.

We know the approximate meaning of this communication, but it doesn't seem to have any bearing on our relationship with horses. They never seem to squeal at us, and I've never yet heard a human squeal at a horse! The volume of the sound, however, *is* of significance. Because horses respect those who make loud noises, a human whose voice is loud is far more likely to instil fear and respect into a horse. Shouting at a badly behaved horse is something humans already do automatically. It is a behaviour we use with each other, so we naturally extend it to our communication with the horse. Similarly, when we wish to be friends with the horse, we speak in a quiet voice. Often men are more respected by horses than are women. In part this is because men tend to have deeper and louder voices.

The soft blow. This sounds as if the horse is blowing his nose. Unlike the hard blow or snort, it means that the horse is relaxed. You wouldn't hear a tense horse making this noise. When you are riding, it is good to hear this sound from him, because it means you are not stressing him and he is ready to begin work. When he blows like this, he is pushing air out of his lungs, showing that they are not tense and are able to work to their maximum.

Do they understand the meaning of noises other horses make?

Of course – there would be no point in making different sounds unless other horses knew why they were making them and that someone else would understand them.

Do they understand the sounds humans make?

No. They cannot recognise words but they can associate certain types of sound with the circumstances in which they heard them. For example a sharp sound, such as "no" when the animal is naughty, may often have been accompanied by a smack. Very quickly, the horse associates "no", said in a harsh way, as a reprimand. When we speak softly to a horse, and stroke it gently at the same time, the horse learns to associate a soft voice with pleasant circumstances. When we are training a horse, "walk on" said in a commanding way, is associated with the dominant status of the trainer. The words themselves are probably not recognised as such, but the feeling behind the words, the tone, the pitch and the combination of pitches is communicated to the horse because of the associations he has with them. For example "walk on" is probably said in two pitches, "walk" being high, "on" being lower, and the "n" being held for a moment longer. It becomes almost musical, and, if repeated in the same way every time that you require the horse to "walk on", he will recognise the command. When you ask the horse to "trot", often you will say this as "terrrrrot". Again, if this sound is repeated when trot is required, it will be recognised. So, if you wish to train your horse by sound, use the same sound and the same intonation or sets of intonations. Accompany the sound by the same actions which ask him to perform the task you require. Repeated often enough, the horse gets to know what you want, merely by recognising what he has heard.

By smell

Horses have a very well developed sense of smell and use it to assess their environment. As for using it for communication, this is probably limited to leaving their droppings for others to know that they have been there.

By behaviour
Sometimes horses give very obvious clues as to their feelings and what they wish to communicate to others, for example:

Swishing tail – He is telling you he is unhappy. It could be a fly or the rider is annoying him.

Flattened ears – "Beware! I'm going to attack you if you don't do as I wish."

Touching noses – "Hello", or "Hello, who are you?", or "I like you!"

Head held low – "I'm not going to hurt you. In fact, I'm probably not here."

Keeping the side of the body facing another animal – "I am very insignificant. I pose no threat to you. I am definitely not here."

Facing another horse with eyes or body – "I am very brave, very superior and not the least bit frightened of you. Do you want to take me on, or are you going to do as I wish?"

A high head carriage – "I'm better than everyone here so don't mess with me."

Quarters angled or turned toward another – "If you don't get out of the way I'll kick you."

Bared teeth – "Go away or I'll bite you."

Clapping the mouth or chewing – "I admit it. You're the boss. I'm nobody. Will you be my friend?"

Pawing the ground – "I'm not too happy", or "I'm going to roll here".

Looking back – Horses who expect to be followed often look back at those they wish to come with them, before they walk on.

Horses also give relatively subtle clues as to their personality or feelings.

No eye contact – "I'm a little afraid of you. If I don't look at you perhaps you won't look at me. Perhaps you won't realise I'm here."

Eye contact is used for communication and tells us what mood the horse is in:

Soft eyes – relaxed happy horse.
Wild eyes with the white showing – frightened horse.
Angry eyes, pleading eyes – other horses will easily pick up on these facial expressions just as we pick up on the look on another person's face. Horses have very expressive faces – sad, contented, quizzical, frightened, frightening or disdainful. We can interpret their facial expressions just as we can with humans. If horses can interpret the facial expressions of other horses, and these are similar to our own, it is possible that they may be able to understand human facial expressions too.
Flared nostrils – they show fear or anger and are associated with the requirement for more oxygen needed for either a fight or a flight.

How do horses listen?
With their ears (surprisingly!) – they will face in the direction, or directions, in which they are listening. They also face their ears in the direction of what they are looking at or concentrating on. It feels as if they are looking at you with their ears. In fact, their peripheral vision is so good that they can see you, even when their head is not turned towards you. By turning their ears towards you they are concentrating their hearing in your direction. When you are riding, if both of the horse's ears are turned back towards you, the horse is concentrating on his work and on what you are telling him to do. He is listening to you, even though you have not made a single noise – your communications have all been physical ones. You then know that you have his attention and concentration.

Can a horse tell you what is wrong with him?
You need to build up a catalogue of his characteristics of behaviour. This helps you to understand his symptoms and make an accurate or a fairly accurate diagnosis. For example, kicking stomach, and/or walking round box looking at stomach, and/or rolling agitatedly – it will probably be

some type of colic. Head hanging low, or not eating, or a temperature – a virus?

Be alert to changes in your horse's behaviour. Remember what has happened in the past to this horse or other horses. Look at the whole horse or feel him under you when he is well. Make a note of it so you can tell the difference when he is not. Make yourself sensitive to his moods, his behaviour and his movement. Then you will be more able to pick up on anything that is wrong, and know when things are not going well and the horse is unhappy.

Particularly notice how your horse greets you, either in the field or the stable. If he normally has his head over the door and greets you with a whinny, you should worry about him if he remains standing in a corner. Similarly, if your horse usually looks up when you call him in the field, and this time he ignores you, perhaps he might have a problem – investigate.

Our communication system – the aids

Riders have created the aids as a method of communicating with horses. Each horse has to be taught what these aids mean. He is not possessed of this knowledge at birth. In creating them we have tried to use sensory signals which are easily understood by the horse.

The aids are given using our hands via the reins, our legs, our backs, our balance and occasionally our voices. It is possible to teach horses to respond to other methods of communication. For example, you *could* teach a horse to canter by pressing with your finger on the right side of the withers for right canter and on the left for left canter. For now, however, we will concentrate on the established aids.

Most of the aids are as they are for obvious practical reasons. For example, when you wish a horse to go to the right, you ask it with the right rein to bring its head to the right, and then the rest of the horse follows. It is easy for us and for the horse to understand. If we wish him to move the whole of his body to the right, we push with our left leg. Again, it is easy for both the horse and ourselves to understand. It is almost the same as getting off the horse and physically pushing him from his left side, so that his whole body moves to the right.

Some of the aids use the laws of physics to help the horse understand what is required, but in each there is an element of association. When he has learnt the meaning of the aid in this way, it will not be long before he does what is required merely because he feels the aid, and knows what it means, rather than waiting for the physical force of the aid. For example if you wish to turn right, and shorten the rein on that side by the smallest amount, he will happily go to the right. You do not have to pull his head over with the right rein as you might have done when he was first ridden. He is doing it because he knows what it means, not because you are forcing him. Gradually you can reduce, and then reduce again the strength of the aid, because the horse still understands what you want of him. The less physical the aid, the less disturbance is caused to the balance and harmony of the horse's movements.

We have to beware of giving the horse signals unconsciously when we do not intend to. He is so adept at picking up on associations. Remember the examples given earlier. He appears to anticipate what we want him to do, because we are doing things we are unaware of, like changing our position and shortening the rein before we canter. Remember to keep your body still while you are riding, until you actually apply the aid.

Horses can understand the body language of other horses, and may interpret our body language, in their own terms. A lowered extended arm looks much like the horse's lowered head, meaning submission or cessation of confrontation. Facing horses frontally is confrontational, whereas the side of our body is not confrontational. If you walk towards a horse, looking into his eyes and facing his body with yours, he regards you as dominant and probably submits to you. If, however, you walked into the stable quietly, with your head down and your body at less than its full height, the horse would know that you were timid and he would probably be able to boss you around. If, every time he moved his quarters in your direction, you leapt away expecting him to kick, he would recognise your nervousness and take advantage of it. Hence a confident, upstanding and/or tall person, who is striding out, is someone to be reckoned with. A person with a lowered head and small steps is someone who can be bossed. A tall person could dominate a horse naturally, whilst a shorter individual has to prove he is not frightened, because instinctively the horse presumes the smaller person to be less strong. A horse regards a person who speaks with a strong voice as someone to be wary of. If we feel confident with horses, it shows in the way we behave and they will know who we are. The horse assesses you as you assess yourself.

12

Dominating Your Horse

If we are to manage horses effectively, we must persuade them that we are their superiors. There must be no question in their minds about this. Though we must treat them fairly, and kindly, this kindness must not extend to softness if you are faced with bad behaviour or disobedience. When you require them to do something, if you know they understand what you require and you know they are capable of achieving it, then you must insist that they do it. This does not mean you should be cruel to them in any way – it merely means that you must not let them get away with any disobedience. If a horse thinks that a rider will tolerate disobedience, this is one of the biggest obstacles to success.

Disciplining horses begins long before you get on their backs. It starts with the way you handle your horse the very first time you meet him, and how you continue from then on. The way you handle him includes the way you walk up to him, how you hold your body, how you look at him and how you touch him. The way you stand and walk, the way you speak to him, the way you groom him, pick his feet out, tack him up, lead him, ride him and most particularly the way in which you deal with naughtiness. You must be confident with him at all times (see Chapter 10). He must know from the way you handle yourself that you are his boss, and are not at all frightened of him.

If he seeks to challenge this domination, you must leave him in no doubt that you will not countenance any challenges! The way in which the horse challenges you will

236

determine the way in which you meet his challenge. When meeting his challenge or his naughtiness, the punishment should fit the crime – if he has tried to, threatened to, or succeeded in kicking or biting you, a very firm whack would fit the bill. If the misdemeanour is less, the punishment also should be less.

Needless to say, all this behaviour on our part is pure bluff. There is no chance that we could physically overpower a horse or make him do as we wish by forcing him. We are play-acting when we are with horses – pretending we are huge and powerful. The way we relate to him must always convince the horse that this is the case. If he ever discovers that it is a bluff, and that he is in fact much stronger, it may become almost impossible to school him.

The way you look at your horse
A subordinate horse would not look a dominant horse directly in the eye for any length of time – this would provoke a confrontation. The more cowardly of the two will avoid this, because he doesn't want the battle. The dominant horse, however, will look the other in the eye because he knows he is boss. Nervous and gentle humans also tend to avoid direct eye contact with other humans, as well as with horses. No wonder horses are so quick to work out which humans are capable of dominating them – innately we use much of the same body language. If you are to be the dominant one in the relationship you must look your horse directly in the eye.

The way you turn your body
If one horse faces another horse with the whole of the front of his body, it is potentially confrontational, just like direct, maintained eye contact. Imagine a subservient horse creeping past a dominant horse. He keeps the side of his body towards the dominant horse, and only looks at him from the corner of his eye. It is as if he can hardly see the dominant horse and is hoping the dominant horse will hardly notice him either. The position of his body makes no confrontation to the other horse, so he is happily ignored. By walking past him in this manner he is saying,

"I am unimportant, I will not be a threat to you, just ignore me".

Imagine a more confident horse who, unafraid of a battle, walks straight up to the other horse face to face, eye to eye. At this point there is either a confrontation, and perhaps a fight, or one of the horses will back down. Most likely the latter.

So, if you turn and face your horse and look him in the eye, he knows you are somebody who is not afraid to confront him. You are in the running to be the boss.

The way you stand

The subservient horse mentioned above probably sidles past the other horse with his head close to the ground. This is to make himself look smaller. The smaller you are the less threatening you are. Imagine the dominant horse standing looking at the subservient horse or perhaps the dominant stallion warding off all comers – he stands as tall as he can make himself, his neck arched and his head high. He wants to look as big as he can, and threatening.

If you want to impress your horse, make yourself appear as big as possible – don't creep past him ignominiously. Take confident strides around him and walk towards him confidently – he will recognise you as a powerful being. If he backs off that is fine. He is a little fearful of you – you are well on the road to being the boss.

The way you speak

When two horses confront each other, the next stage of the meeting may be a squealing competition. The squeal is one of the loudest noises a horse makes. The horse who makes the loudest squeal may be accepted as the victor in the battle for dominance. We humans don't enter into the squealing contest, but we can assert our superiority by speaking with a strong voice when we wish the horse to recognise us as the dominant partner. Conversely, if we wish to be his friend, we can speak softly.

It is worth noting at this point the reasons why men often manage to win the respect of horses where a woman fails. Consider the (usually) greater physical strength of a man, his greater size and deeper, louder voice. This is more respected by the horse, who has learnt from experience that the larger and noisier the potential threat, the more dangerous it is likely to be. It could also be that women tend to be gentler and kinder to horses, which is a trait that the horse would recognise as a weakness

Once having won respect from the horse, you will find him all the more eager to bond and become your friend. The horse recognises that having such a powerful person for a friend is very much to his advantage. He will be appreciative of the love and care you show him. This combination of power and affection creates the strongest bond possible.

The way you handle him

This is when the horse really weighs you up as a character. How do you touch him? How do you brush him? If your handling of him is confident and easy, not nervous and hesitant, he knows you do not fear him and, therefore, perhaps he may treat you with caution.

If, on the other hand, you are nervous, tense, and perhaps over gentle, he suspects that he can push you around. Few horses can resist the temptation of taking a nervous person for a ride – figuratively speaking of course!

The way you manage his naughtiness

There are very, very few saintly horses who never bite, kick, paw the ground or mess about. The vast majority challenge your authority at some time. They are testing the ground to see how you will respond. If you do nothing, or little, they will probably take it a little further and be a little naughtier. Before you know where you are, you could have a thoroughly badly behaved horse on your hands and not because the horse is bad, but because you are useless at teaching him how to respect you.

There is, sadly, only one way that I know of to deal with bad behaviour – just as the mother would reprimand her foal when he steps out of line, you must reprimand your charge when he misbehaves. A small smack will be ignored; it must be sufficiently hard for the horse not to wish to invite a recurrence of the punishment by misbehaving again. A firm smack will be respected. Anything much more than this will have a detrimental effect on your relationship, and is to be abhorred if it reflects violence or cruelty in any way. If you have to smack your horse, avoid doing this on his head. Because of the eyes and the delicate tissue of the head, it is easy to physically damage your horse by hitting him here and even easier to create a head shy horse. (A head shy horse is one who nervously lifts his head into the air every time you lift your hand towards it.) A punishment must be administered immediately so that the horse can relate it to his wrongdoing. If there is any kind of gap it will cause the horse a lot of confusion and upset, because he will not remember what it was for. The shoulders, the neck, the quarters and behind the girth are normal areas to administer punishment. Where you will administer it will depend on your location in relation to the horse at the time of the misdemeanour. You can smack with your open hand as it creates a lot of noise, but beware, it can hurt you a good deal more than it does the horse. A riding stick or whip, used once, is often more effective.

It is difficult to say exactly where or with what you should discipline your horse. It is something that has to be done immediately and therefore the part of the horse that is nearest at the time is the most available. Preferably it would also involve that part of the horse that has committed the offence. This will help him understand what the punishment is for. It is unwise to hit your horse if standing behind him. He may decide to retaliate and you would be in a very vulnerable position. If you were holding a riding stick, you would use that, or if you were not, you use your hand. Do not lose the moment by going to get a stick. The horse may forget the connection between the crime and the punishment and will regard your behaviour as cold blooded.

When you smack your horse, discipline him with your voice at the same time. If you always do this, after a while you will only need to shout at him and it will be sufficient to make him feel suitably punished. Some horses are sensitive and will not need a physical reprimand. A verbal admonishment will be all they need to understand that you are displeased with them. Anything more would be cruel and probably make them frightened and tense.

Sometimes the bad behaviour occurs when the horse is being ridden – for example, a rear or a buck. This is difficult to deal with. You know that, if you smack your horse, you are probably inviting more of the same from him. You are, quite justifiably, frightened of being hurt if he throws you off. Instead of smacking your horse, you could try riding him forwards very strongly. If he obeys your leg and goes forwards, you have won the argument. If he disobeys your leg and repeats the buck or rear, you must punish your horse. A firm smack behind the leg with the riding stick will let him know you are not happy with him. He will probably buck or rear again and you will have to smack him again. At this point most horses give up and start to behave themselves. Enforcing horse discipline may well test your riding ability, and certainly your nerve, but, thankfully, once you have established yourself as his boss, your horse will misbehave less and less frequently. When your horse has done as you asked him, be sure to remember to praise him – give him every reason to behave well.

Most horses give up when they recognise you are not going to be bullied or frightened by them. It is down to your bravery, and whether you mind the possibility of falling off. The problem with not taking that risk is that the horse will know that he is boss. You are frightened of him and he can do what he likes. At this point, some people send their horse away for schooling (to someone who is not afraid). Unfortunately, the problem is a personal one between you and your horse. Another person may well be able to stop him bucking or rearing, but when the horse comes home he recognises you, and remembers that you were the coward who didn't stand up to him. If this is your case, perhaps you would be better selling this horse and buying a more amenable animal.

Remember: when chastising the horse, the voice should be used at the same time as any other form of reprimand. If this is done every time the horse needs discipline, he will associate the voice with punishment. The voice may ultimately suffice on its own as a punishment, without the need for anything more.

The play-acting described above is not necessarily for ever. When you have established your relationship, and he knows you are dominant, you can normally relax into a gentler way of living with each other without the need to be constantly asserting your supremacy. Occasionally, though, the horse (depending on his character) may seek an opportunity to test this – just be ready to deal with it as before.

More serious bad behaviour
Some people say that bad horses are made, not born. Usually this is true, but there are some horses, though thankfully precious few, who are born determined to be the boss. They seek to establish their dominance in the way that they would in the herd – by violence. They will kick and bite, rear and buck in an attempt to boss you. This would be fine if they were being left out in the field and never ridden. But it is unacceptable if, every time you want to ride them, they again try to re-establish their dominance – by not letting you catch them, by rearing, biting or kicking. Thankfully there really are very few animals who are like this naturally, but it is easy for horses like this to be created through their owner's mishandling. If you have a horse who manifests these tendencies, there is only one way forward. That is, to be prepared to prove to him that you can dominate him.

A word of warning – do not attempt to handle really violent horses unless you are very experienced, competent and confident with horses. Some (though very, very few) can be mean, nasty and potentially dangerous. In these circumstances the trainer assumes a role similar to that of a lion tamer! It is a dangerous job and one for a professional who has nerves of steel and knows exactly what he is doing.

If your horse bites or kicks you, or threatens to do either of these things, there is rarely any choice for you but to smack him. This is the language of the herd. You are telling him you are not afraid of him and if he hurts you, or tries to, you will hurt him more. It seems awful that a book, whose ethos is one of gentleness, love and kindness to the horse, recommends hitting them, but now you are talking horse language. This is how they seek dominance in the herd and it is how you must establish dominance now. You must have an ultimate punishment available to use on a badly behaved horse. There has to be a reason for the horse to do as he is told.

If you are nervous you have a problem. You must become an actor. Pretend to be confident. Follow all the rules set out for convincing your horse that you are the boss. However, it may be that the horse has already evaluated your personality, and knows he can intimidate you. It is, therefore, doubly difficult for you to convince him that your character and confidence have changed overnight, but this is what you must do. The best way to do it is to shell-shock him into believing you have changed, by making yourself very theatrically dominant. Everything you do must be over-the-top. Make a lot of noise when you go into the stable. If the horse puts a foot out of line, be very, very firm with him. You must become so utterly dominant that he will believe you really have changed. After you have convinced him, and his behaviour starts to improve, you can reduce the play acting, but you must never stop it altogether. If you were to slip back into the same intimidated person as before, he will quickly realise and start to take advantage again. He will value you as you value yourself – that is, as his subordinate.

There is often a metamorphosis when a badly behaved horse is sent away for schooling. He arrives at the trainer's yard, and is instantly better behaved. The reason is that the horse is phased by the new surroundings and people. At first he tries to work out where he belongs in the hierarchy, and behaves well, at least until he has worked out whom, if anyone, he can boss around and whom he can't. The people there are professionals and not the least intimidated by him. He knows this from their body language and how they handle him. Throughout his time there he will behave because they are dominant, and he has to do as he is told. When his schooling has finished, he is returned to his owner a changed horse – for about two days. It won't be long before the horse remembers his old owner and behaves just as he did before. The moral of this story – perhaps it is the owner who should go away for schooling!

You may think that being so firm with your horse is cruel, but it is the opposite. Once your horse knows you are the boss, he relaxes in your company. He finds strength in your strength and this makes him secure and happy. Just like children, horses need discipline, without which they would be unhappy, difficult creatures. Remember that to be a successful rider, just as to be a successful parent, you need to be strong enough to be firm. True affection from your horse is engendered from the knowledge that he is secure in your strong but caring company. Animals roaming freely in the wild attach themselves to a strong friend. In exactly the same way your horse will attach himself to you because he perceives that you will fend off all attackers and look after him. The fact that you feed him as well, and are kind to him when he is good, serves to reinforce this dependency and the desire to keep you as his friend by doing as you ask.

13

Reward or Punishment?

Positive reinforcement

Traditionally, the attitude of the horse training industry is: if the horse does as he is asked, everything is fine. If he doesn't, he will be punished. In other words, horses are trained by punishment or fear. The whip is often to hand and we expect horses to be scared of it.

The alternative method of training is by positive reinforcement. The horse is praised when he does things correctly, and given a reward. The advantage of positive reinforcement is that, because pleasant things happen during training sessions, the whole atmosphere changes. Instead of being filled with dread, it becomes a happy time that the horse can look forward to. Both horse and rider share this benevolent feeling and, because the horse is enjoying his work, he should perform better.

The rewards you can give your horse vary. You might give him a rest, or stroke his neck. Stopping work altogether is the greatest reward. You can also praise him with your voice. Some are against it, but giving the horse a titbit is easily understood, and welcome as a reward, though there are potential problems. The horse may come to expect to be given something. He could develop bad habits such as stopping of his own accord or, when stopped, reach towards your hand with his mouth. Some horses are particularly prone to this but your horse can be trained to wait for you to offer the reward rather than demand it. Simply use the aid to go on a little more assertively, when he is thinking about stopping. Keep a firm hold on the reins if he begins to reach towards you. This should be adequate to convey your intention to him.

This morning my very mischievous kitten was up to high jinks in the bedroom. I was going out, so, before I could put the alarm on, I had to put the kitten out. The morning before, I had been in the same situation and tried to chase him out of the room. He had darted everywhere and it took me several minutes before I finally got him out. The result: a defeated, unhappy cat and a tired me. This morning, another approach. Walking out of the room I called "puss, puss", in very much the same kind of voice as I would use to tell him there was food being served. The kitten, anticipating something nice, followed me out immediately. The moral of the story: always try to get your way without a fight, and try and keep the ending happy!

If you use these kinds of technique with your horse, life is much easier and more pleasant. Don't meet him head on, waiting for a fight. Use your brain and find the easy way round. Look for the best way to teach something. Last year a friend told me her horse became quite silly every time she asked it to do half pass. He should have found this manoeuvre quite easy, but he didn't and got distressed when asked for it. She could have carried on asking him to do it, using stronger and stronger aids, but this would probably have made him more upset. Instead, she went back to a very similar but easier exercise – leg yielding. The horse had no problem with this so she asked him to do this exercise during every schooling session. When she was sure he was relaxed and happy with leg yielding, she slightly changed the angle of his body bit by bit, until he was doing half pass without any fuss or worry.

The principles of learning
Some of the answers you seek may be found in this section, but there can never be a comprehensive guide on how to do it. There is too wide a variety of situations and too many difficult kinds of horse. It is up to you to use your brains all the time to work out the best solution.

When your horse has worked for you, and given more

than he has before, make a big fuss of him and perhaps stop work. He will know this is a reward and horses have such good memories that he will not forget. Fill his mind full with good associations and memories when he does well for you. Soon he will learn that pleasing you is one of the best things in the world. It is wonderful when, every time you take him out and train him, he regards it as a treat.

Punishment

Occasionally you have to administer discipline or punishment. There are invariably times when he misbehaves or is disobedient. Minimise these occasions and keep the relationship between you sweet. Don't ever let a schooling session finish on a bad note. If your horse has been really unco-operative and difficult, ask him to do something you know he will do well, and then praise or reward him. Either do this again or find something else he will do well. Again praise or reward him. Finish the lesson there. If he has done as he is told, and felt good about it, he will remember this the next time you school him. Get him into the habit of always doing as he is told and always feeling good about it because he has been rewarded. As long as you do not ask him to do anything that is difficult for him, and proceed slowly with his training, you need never stray far from this philosophy.

There are other times when you can use positive reinforcement as a training aid to good effect. Imagine the horse who hates having his girth tightened (or perhaps I should say *her* girth tightened, mares being what they are). The horse may snap at you, or flinch, or lift a leg in half threat. Naughty though this behaviour is, the horse does it because of hatred or fear of the tightened girth. If we now get angry and smack him, or shout at him if he registers his displeasure, his dislike or fear is reinforced because of your scolding.

Instead of being cross, try to understand how he feels. Just before and while you tighten the girth, stroke your horse and talk to him nicely. Perhaps give him a titbit. Try to help him forget about the discomfort of the girth and only think about the pleasant things that are happening to him. If you repeat this every time the girth is tightened, eventually he should associate it with desirable sensations. Ultimately you should be able to make less and less fuss of him as his dislike for the girth is tempered. You have put a happy association in the place of an unpleasant experience.

On the road
Some horses have a nervous disposition. Some situations make them even more nervous and tense, riding out on the road, for example. Obviously this makes them unsafe in traffic. Because they are nervous, they misbehave: jumping out from things in the hedge or swinging their quarters into the path of vehicles. Then the rider often gets nervous too, and may often get cross with the horse. It sounds like stating the obvious, but, if you get cross with a nervous horse, all you get is a more nervous and badly behaved one. A calm rider does far more for this type of horse. If you can give the horse something else to think about while he is on the road, you may be able to take his mind off what is upsetting him. A series of transitions – walk, trot, walk, halt, trot, etc. are very useful. Riding your horse along the left-hand side of the road, turn his head very slightly to the right. To stop him from walking into the road, keep your right leg against his side and a firm contact on your left rein. This keeps him mentally occupied, and in a safe outline when traffic is approaching. When the horse's head is turned a little to the right, his right eye can see behind him. Traffic coming up behind him is seen with this eye. If it frightens him, this makes him move away from it, safely towards the road's verge. If he sees the traffic coming from the rear with his left eye, he will move away from it to the right, which takes him out into the middle of the road. When the traffic does pass by, talk to him in a calm reassuring voice.

When you are riding, avoid tension in your own body. If you are nervous, the horse will pick up on it. If you are frightened, he will think there is reason for him to be frightened also. Relax your body so as to let him know you are not nervous (even if you are). This helps him to relax because he feels the relaxation in your body. If you find it difficult to relax, sing a song to yourself.

If you are riding past something which makes the horse nervous, do not make him look at it. This only makes him become more nervous. Keep his head away from it. Try and pretend that it doesn't exist or, even if it does, it is nothing to make a fuss about. There is a good chance the horse will believe you.

Use a horse's reaction to frequent exposure to make him better behaved on the road. Taking horses out every day for a week, using the same stretch of road, should make them less nervous of what they encounter there. If a horse has been frightened of something he hears or sees in the roadside, but is never hurt by, he learns to ignore it. If, however, the rider scolds the horse when he jumps away in fright, then by hurting his horse, the rider has reinforced his horse's fear. The horse feels justified in being frightened of what is in the roadside because, as an indirect result of it, he has felt pain.

Don't reward bad behaviour

You may be teaching your horse a new or difficult exercise when he becomes nervous and tense. It could be that he is struggling to cope with understanding or performing what you want. Often, when the horse gets tense and disobedient, the rider gets cross and the horse gets even tenser. This is counterproductive. It creates a bad memory for the horse, linked to this particular work. Try to keep calm and think of another easier way to teach the lesson. The horse should also remain calm, and learn the lesson with no bad associations. It may take a little longer than you had hoped, but the benefits are many.

There are times when you take your horse out to train him and he is badly behaved. He will not settle to work, or will not do as you ask him. It could be because the horse is tense, but, whatever the reason, it is a bad idea to stop work because of this. If you do, you are teaching him to associate being bad with earning a rest and reward. No matter how badly he behaves (and very often it can seem pointless carrying on), you must keep going. You know your horse. Find something he likes to do, or does easily.

Do this until his behaviour improves, then give him a rest or a reward. If it doesn't improve, don't give him the reward he expects. For example, suppose that, after work, he usually goes out with the other horses. Instead of this, put him on his own in the stable, or don't give him hay and a feed. Later bring him out and ride him some more. Again, do something he will find easy. Don't confront him. This time you hope he will do something that is worthy of praise. Seize on this, make a fuss of him, and give him his reward. He must never be given a reward for bad behaviour, only for good. Keep on with this system until the penny drops.

Naughtiness?

One of the most difficult problems one is confronted with when schooling horses is disobedience. Is the horse being naughty, or doesn't he understand what you have asked him to do? Perhaps he is physically incapable of performing the task, or finds it physically difficult. Perhaps the horse has become tense and this makes him unable to settle down to his work. To know how to deal with his disobedience, you need to know the reason for it. If you are totally sure he is being naughty, it isn't a problem. If he were being demonstrably naughty – bucking, rearing or kicking – a smack would be in order. Smacking a nervous horse, though, even if he has appeared naughty, is always counterproductive. It makes him even more nervous. He may not recover during that schooling session. You need to know why he is behaving as he is. If he is merely not doing as you ask, repeat the request until he does it.

Some horses, particularly intelligent mares, resent being disciplined unjustifiably. If they have done something wrong, they do not mind being punished. If they have been trying to accomplish something and have not been able to – because either they don't understand or they have a physical difficulty – their punishment in such circumstances can easily destroy any trust the horse may have in you, and damage your relationship. Some horses – particularly geldings – will apparently cope with unreasoned discipline well, but even so it must confuse them.

There are times when you are sure he is misbehaving – a naughty toss of the head, perhaps a buck, whatever; you know your own horse and can tell when he is definitely being naughty. In this case a smack is appropriate. But then if you are not sure . . . you wonder whether to scold him or whether to force him to repeat the movement. You wonder if your explanation has not been clear to the horse and if you should try again. There is a simple answer. Presume the latter: presume you got it wrong, not the horse, and explain it more carefully this time. Unless you are absolutely sure he is being disobedient you must presume confusion or physical difficulty. Otherwise you risk a fight with your horse which you may not win. Whatever the cause, he will be left with unpleasant memories, and perhaps unfortunate associations with the movement forever. You may feel that failure to punish him for a disobedience is letting him get away with it. In fact, because you are asking him to repeat the movement, this is not so. He will think that his bad behaviour wasn't worth the effort, because it made no difference. Despite his protest you are still making him do what he didn't want to.

When you re-explain it to him, imagine at the same time that he finds it physically difficult to do. Your task now is to go through the back door to his senses, his intelligence and his physical ability. Don't meet him head on ready for an argument and a fight. Ask him to do something easy, that is perhaps similar to what you want. Praise him and reward him with a pat. Make a big fuss of him. Explain really clearly what you want, and ask him to do ever such a little bit of it. Praise him, and reward him even if he accomplishes it only half well. Keep your patience. Losing your temper with animals never works to your advantage in the end. "Softly, softly catchee monkey." Keep your horse happy and wanting to please you. Before you know it, he will be doing what you want, because he wants to earn your praise and a reward. Your own reward will be a happy horse who will work so much harder for you. Once you have gentled your way through one problem, all others diminish, because you have learnt to work, play and have fun with your horse rather than to fight him.

Inevitably it will sometimes be necessary to scold your horse for disobedience. When it is necessary, do not shirk it. Be firm, and brave. You have to know you can deal with any worse action or revenge your horse may take as a result of the punishment. If you are nervous he will know. He must believe you are the boss. So, if you have to correct disobedience, be very firm, make it immediate and make it totally obvious why he has done wrong. Don't lose your temper and overdo the punishment: you may destroy his trust in you as a friend. Don't make the punishment too little: he will ignore it. Don't nag: this results when the punishment is insignificant to the horse and he ignores it. You end up repeating it, never as strongly as necessary. He learns to ignore it totally, because nothing worse happened when it was ignored. Frequent exposure again. Any punishment, if it must be given, must have sufficient impact that the horse will not want it repeated.

But, where possible, school your horse by reward, not punishment. Progress will be much faster and more fun.

14

The Temperament of Horses

Horses are all different

Horses come in a variety of mentalities. They are just as diverse as human beings. Some are cowardly, some nervous, some tense and some dominant. Others are gentle, high-spirited, brave or lazy. Some are affectionate, some brutish, some sensible and calm, while others are skittish or stupid. There is no such thing as an average horse. They are not machines built to an exact physical and mental design. They all have their quirks, their weaknesses, their hang-ups and their strengths. Therefore, if we are to school horses intelligently, we need to understand, not only the physiology and psychology of horses in general, but also the individual physique and mentality of each horse we school. We must use our intelligence to work out a way of schooling that suits them as individuals.

Horses change

Never stop re-evaluating your horse. As you school him, his mind and body develops and changes. Mentally and physically, he becomes a different being. As he changes you must be aware of the metamorphosis and constantly rethink your schooling methods. That which would work two months ago may not work today! Remember also that horses' moods can change a lot with the seasons, in the case of mares with their cycles, and for all horses with the weather and their food. They also develop and change as they age and mature. Horses also alter in character and sometimes in temperament as their training progresses. Hence this examination of their character is not a static thing. It needs to be constantly re-assessed.

Males v females

There are general and well-known differences between mares, geldings and stallions. There is an expression – you tell a gelding, ask a mare and discuss it with a stallion. Needless to say, this is a generalisation, but by and large geldings are more laid back and will cope with being pushed around, and even a bit of unfair treatment. They are relatively easy to deal with. Mares, however, are more sensitive, and will resent a rough or unthinking rider. A lot of people won't have mares for this reason. But the truth is that, if you are unable to handle a mare, you really aren't such a good rider. They require tact and caring riding which some people, most particularly impatient men, cannot cope with. If a mare is unjustifiably punished she will be very upset and let her rider know it. If a mare is rewarded for good work she will repay you twice over in her efforts to please you. Being female myself I can quite empathise and sympathise with this behaviour. There is another saying that a bad mare is the worst horse, but a good mare is the best. I am sure this is also true, so long as their riders are capable of bringing out the best in them.

Delve deeper into their characters

A trainer must recognise what type his horse is, so that he knows how to deal with him and get the best out of him. Each horse has a basic temperament type, which is often easy to spot, but also he will have other quirks, likes and dislikes which may take a little time to work out. Take some time to study him, his reactions and his manners. Examine his personality and behaviour under a microscope, so that you know how he, as an individual, will take to the training you give him. If you know him well you can adapt your training to suit him and also be ready for what may happen. Preparation will help you to deal with potentially difficult situations.

Horses can be slow-witted or intelligent, lazy or energetic, tense or calm, affectionate, unaffectionate or nasty, well-mannered or ill-mannered, confident or sensitive. These basic temperaments are the core of the horse's personality and rarely change during his life. We can mould their behaviour through training but underneath they are still the same personality. A nasty horse can be taught manners and a lazy horse can be made to perform with more energy, but all the time we are fighting against nature – the job of moulding them is hard and their basic personality will often rise to the surface.

Slow learners: Some horses aren't very intelligent. Where another horse might understand a lesson immediately, they don't. If you know your horse is dull-witted and slow learning, you will need more patience when you teach him a new lesson. Rather than losing your patience, you must think of other ways of getting him to do as you wish, ways that won't stress his brain too much. You are his teacher. Like all good teachers, you must find the best way of communicating your information to your pupil.

Quick learners: If he learns lessons quickly, and is easily bored, keep his brain occupied and stretched. Be careful not to put strain on his body by making the lessons too advanced if he is mentally further ahead then he is physically.

Nervous horses: If you know your horse is nervous, you will realise that there is no mileage in getting cross with him – you will send him crazy. Instead you must teach him calmly and avoid doing anything that might set off his tension. Read in the chapter on tension the ways in which you can help him to be more relaxed.

Lazy horses: It is very frustrating riding a horse that plods slowly wherever it goes. They will only trot after a lot of effort from the rider's legs and then it is often a slow trot. Canter is another thing altogether – almost impossible! Increasing the level of concentrated feed and cutting down on the amount of hay or grass may make these animals more energetic. An energetic rider may also help by constantly demanding more from him and never accepting his natural slowness.

Energetic horses: They love to move fast and, as long as they aren't tense, are a joy to ride. Some of these horses can become impatient when you ask them to work more slowly, particularly in situations where there are other horses passing them. If their speed and enthusiasm is a problem, it may help if you reduce their concentrated feed. It may also be worthwhile considering using a stronger bit.

Affectionate, unaffectionate or nasty horses: Horses are often born either affectionate or unaffectionate but their treatment by humans can make a difference. If a horse has been deprived of affection, he will become withdrawn and unable to give it. This situation can be reversed when a human gives time, love and attention to his horse. It is also important that the horse holds his handler in respect. You would rarely engender love and affection from a horse that is undisciplined. Inevitably there are horses that are unaffectionate or nasty by nature and no amount of love, attention and/or discipline would induce them to return it.

Well-mannered and ill-mannered horses: You may well think that the manners of the horse lie in the discipline and training that he is given. For the most part you would be right, but some horses are born with good manners. They never barge past you or stand on your toes or drag you out of the stable. They stop when you stop and carefully walk around you if you are in the way. Then there are the horses who never seem to know or care where their feet are. If they want to go somewhere, they just go, and if someone is in the way, they just blast through them or over them and never round them. Yes, they can be improved through training, but there will still be an occasion when they forget and trample you or drag you in their enthusiasm to get where they are going.

Confident horses: There are some horses that feel good about themselves and about life. They don't worry a great deal, little seems to frighten them and they are happy taking on new situations and challenges.

Sensitive horses: Some horses can be phased by the big occasions like a large show. This sensitivity is normally manifested by nervousness but some horses become quiet and withdrawn and are not able to give their best. The more they experience these occasions, the less it affects them and the quicker they will feel at ease. Be aware that some horses do not show tension but bottle it up inside them. On the surface they appear to be calm, sensible creatures but underneath all is turmoil. If your horse might fit into this category, give him as much time and consideration as you would give an outwardly tense horse.

Some horses are sensitive to being pressured in their work. Even though they may be physically capable of doing the work, they cannot cope with the mental strain. Others get upset if they are shouted at or smacked unjustifiably. They may show this sensitivity by becoming tense or by being withdrawn. It is often difficult to tell how much work horses can cope with, so it is always wise to "make haste slowly" with them.

Many horses are upset when they move home. It takes them a while to settle in the new and strange environment. Meanwhile they can be quiet and unhappy. Such horses need to be treated particularly kindly and sympathetically during this time. Extra attention will help them settle in. They need to make friends, both equine and human, so offer your friendship and bond with them. Such horses settle better when they know the routine of their new home, and also know where they fit into the hierarchy of their human and equine companions. It is also a time to take advantage of their insecurity, by showing them the standards of behaviour you require, right at the beginning. It is much easier to become the boss at this time. Just as a new member in a club is given the rules when he joins, so must you give your horse a list of rules when he enters the new environment. It is relatively easy to establish behaviour at first, but becomes increasingly difficult to change later what has become established.

Match horse to rider
The temperament of the rider should complement the temperament of the horse. If you are a timid rider, you should not ride a dominant or a high spirited horse. He would either dominate you or frighten you to death. If you are a laid back rider, you should not ride a lazy horse. You will get nowhere slowly. You should ride a horse with energy. Conversely, if you have a fiery or energetic temperament, you would not be well matched on a fiery or energetic horse. The two of you would go everywhere at a hundred miles an hour!

I remember a pony, a beautiful chestnut mare, bought for our daughter, who was then about 11 years old. It was a high spirited and nervous animal and my daughter was intent on success. She was motivated and forward thinking. She was constantly being run away with by the pony and in the end we had to decide to sell her. We thought finding a suitable home for her would be impossible, and that she would need a strong, competent rider. We were astounded when a small, gentle child came to try her and instantly transformed the pony into a gentle, calm creature. The two became a strong and loving partnership. The pony just needed love, and gentle handling, which our daughter at that stage of her life wasn't able to give her.

Teaching methods to suit the horse
Your teaching regime should match the pupil. If he is easily bored, keep him interested with varied lessons. If he learns lessons really quickly, teach him more. If he finds concentrating for a long time hard, keep the lessons short. If he is excitable, make the lessons boring so that he will settle. If he is a stubborn animal who refuses to do something, and you wish to avoid a stand up battle, find a way to trick him into doing it without his realising. You could also try this approach if he is wilful and disobedient. But if it doesn't work, you will need to stand up to him fearlessly and make him know he has to do as you wish.

The list of different temperaments is almost inexhaustible. You must use your own brain to work out who your horse is, and how you should handle him best.

A happy horse

Your horse's state of mind is crucial. A happy horse who cares for his rider, and feels his rider cares for him, will perform much better than the horse who is made to perform grudgingly. Strive to build up a trusting relationship with one another by treating him fairly and not over-straining him. Make your time together fun. He should always be your friend, and he should know it. He should want to do what you want. What a horse learns to do happily he enjoys more, and therefore gives more effort and performs better. When you are schooling, reward and rest frequently. If there is strain, discomfort or shouting, or anything else unpleasant, the horse associates this with what you are asking him to do, and may never do it happily or to his best. Unpleasant memories remain with him for a long time, and spoil that work with which he associates them. Try and inject pleasure into what you are doing. Whenever you can, steer away from discomfort, strain or pain. Avoid punishment unless it is absolutely necessary.

Imagine a child having piano lessons who was shouted at, criticised and whose knuckles were rapped. Compare this to a child who was praised often, rarely scolded, and whose teacher made the lessons fun. Even if the first child is motivated to be a pianist, that desire is soon knocked out of him. He makes no extra efforts for the tutor. His playing lacks inspiration and joy. It has been forced out of the child. You know it when you hear him playing. The child taught kindly, however, takes pleasure in learning new lessons, and seeks to please the tutor. This child's playing reflects the joy he finds in the music.

So is it with horses. A bullied horse performs grudgingly. He lacks the inspiring and energetic movement that should reflect the joy he has found in performing well and pleasing his rider. You have more chance of finding this in a horse ridden by a caring, thinking rider. He makes the lessons less arduous, and more pleasant, by praising and rewarding the horse, and by not being over-demanding.

The confidence and respect which we hope to achieve from our horse does not come easily. It has to be worked for. Your brain has to work overtime on ways to keep him working happily. But it is not just as easy as that. You also have to earn his respect and his obedience. Combining these two is not so straightforward.

This relationship will be stretched to its limit at times when you have to push your horse to work harder than he feels he wants to. Above all, he is an athlete, and the training of an athlete is demanding. You have to remember that, without pain, there is often no gain, and balance it with the knowledge of just how far you can take it. Try and make every schooling session fun. Avoid over tiring, over-stressing, over-straining or boring your horse. Particularly avoid getting cross or losing your temper with him. Keep your training interesting and varied, and praise and rest your horse frequently. Your horse should look forward to the next schooling session – he should never dread it. If the work you are doing is particularly hard or stressful, don't make the lesson last for too long. A tiny achievement can sometimes be enough. Just occasionally a lesson may need to be long if he is struggling to understand what you want. Perhaps you could explain it better to him, or maybe there is no other way but to slog on. If this does happen, make it the exception, otherwise your lessons will be anticipated as periods of torture.

It is possible to achieve quite a lot in a short time, either because the horse is naturally talented and athletic, or by demanding a lot of him. A horse has to work at his own pace, which is determined by his natural mental and physical ability. If you can understand your horse and what he is trying to tell you, it should be apparent how much work he can cope with. If he is pushed too hard, he has no joy in his work because he associates it with discomfort. When you are working your horse, be aware of how he is feeling. Always listen to what he is trying to say to you.

No pain no gain

There is, needless to say, a flip side to this sympathetic, gentle way of training. Developing your horse's athletic ability is something he does not find easy. The degree of difficulty depends partly on his own natural ability and partly on the level to which you wish to take him. It is comparable to a body builder trying to improve his physique in a gym, or perhaps the gruelling training of a ballet dancer. It may involve many, many hours of hard, repetitive work. If you wish to do this work in the gym or become a ballet dancer, the motivation is already there. It is your decision. But, it was not your horse's decision to take on this degree of work, He is not always as keen as you might be to achieve the end goal, nor on the work that will take him there. Inevitably, then, there are times when he finds the work hard and resents it, and so there must be times when you will have to push him where he doesn't want to go. It is then that you have to use all your skill and tact to persuade him to carry on. It may be hard for him but, unless you are prepared to make him, and unless he is prepared to do it, he will not progress beyond his current level. It is at times like these, and there may be many of them, that your domination has to be asserted and followed through. He has to know you are the boss.

When muscles have to be worked hard to develop strength, and when the body has to be stretched, it is hard for him and you have to insist. So much slogging has to take place to improve the performance – it is often tough and very tedious, with great gaps when nothing seems to be achieved at all. If your horse has developed trust in you, he is more inclined to do as you ask when you have to ask him to work hard. He knows you do not drive him unmercifully on when he is aching, tired and uncomfortable. When you hit one of these schooling sessions, whisper to your horse "no pain no gain". If he trusts you, and if he is listening to you, your relationship will hopefully continue unscathed. What you achieve is a horse that feels himself so much your partner that he wants what you want. Your joy becomes his joy, your achievement his achievement!

15

Tension

Tension is part of the temperament of horses but it is such a big item it deserves a chapter of its own.

A tense mind
A tense horse can never produce his best work. This particularly applies to dressage and showing, but it is also important in other equestrian spheres. He is too wound up with his tension to concentrate properly on what he is doing, or on what you are asking him to do. At the least it can be distracting. At the worst it can totally ruin his performance, send him haywire and possibly make him dangerous. To do his job properly he must be relaxed. It is just as important to have a relaxed horse when you are training him as when you are at competitions. Perhaps you need a calm horse even more when you are riding out on the roads. If your horse is constantly spooking at real or imaginary things in the hedge or elsewhere, it makes your ride both unpleasant and dangerous. When he leaps out away from what frightens him, he may well leap into the path of a passing car.

A tense body
If a horse is tense in his mind, he is also tense in his body. A tense body cannot use itself properly because it is not relaxed. The horse must be relaxed if he is to be athletic. The tension makes his body stiff, and hence lack the flexibility it needs in order to work properly. Each muscle

and ligament is tight and constricted. The back is rigid, inflexible and possibly hunched. Each step is short and staccato. Tension totally mars the physical performance of any horse. A tense body can never perform well, or anywhere near its maximum.

Different types of tension

Most horses, when stressed, become jumpy and tense. Some manifest their tension by becoming faster in their work, rushing everything they do. Some become irritable and their character changes. They flatten their ears and threaten to bite when, otherwise, they would be sweet natured. Occasionally horses who are stressed "go into themselves", becoming unusually quiet and unmotivated. These horses often hang well back in company, and go much more slowly than usual.

Causes of tension

The nature of the horse

Some horses are tense by nature. It is difficult, or impossible, to change these horses and make them any less tense. However, you can capitalise on certain equine tendancies. For example, most horses are calmer in an environment in which they feel safe, and less calm in unfamiliar places. By frequently exposing them to the unfamiliar environment, they may grow to regard it as a familiar one, and relax.

A show ground may be something new for your horse. When he is there, he may be tense and therefore under-perform. You could keep away from all shows because of this. A tense horse at a show is both frightening and depressing. But, if you want him to get used to shows, make a particular point of going to as many as you can. Make the gap between shows as short as possible. After six or so shows you should find that your horse begins to regard them as familiar, and becomes less tense. If you didn't compete in the first few shows, this would be a further reason for the horse to relax. Try and remember, while there, to be calm yourself. A horse's tension easily passes onto the rider, and then back to the horse. It becomes a vicious circle of tension which only you can break.

Horses who have been made tense

Pain, fear, and fear of pain are all very potent, and understandable, causes of tension. If a horse has been frightened or hurt, then he will be tense when confronted with the cause of the fear or hurt again. He could be remembering an accident, or perhaps he has been over-faced at a jump. Because of their incredible memories, it is difficult to make horses understand that the same things will not happen again. You have to teach your horse that these situations are no longer dangerous. You achieve this by repeatedly exposing him to similar circumstances and being sure that nothing horrible happens. The horse comes to realise that his fears are no longer justified. For example, if a horse has been over-faced, by jumping too high, he may have become frightened of all jumps. If he can now be persuaded to jump over tiny obstacles, he begins to realise that there are some jumps he can manage. It is better to jump several small jumps, six or seven times over a week or two. Let it really sink in that he can manage to do it and that nothing awful is going to happen to him when he does. Only jump a few jumps each time. Make a big fuss of him after he has jumped. Teach him to associate jumping with pleasure. Hopefully the memory of the pain or fear will go away. Later on, you can gradually increase the height of the jumps, taking care to avoid over-facing him again.

Large jumps, or the possibility of pain, are not the only things that can frighten horses. Difficult or strenuous flat work can be too demanding, and can cause them to fear all work on the flat. If the horse is otherwise calm until you start to school him on the flat, presume that something too strenuous has been asked of him. Try asking the horse to perform only very easy tasks for a week or two, keeping the lessons short and fun, and rewarding the horse after-wards. This should help cure his fear of flat work.

If you can remember what work you had done before the tension occurred, and what had actually caused the tension, you can prevent its recurrence. It is probable that the horse wasn't strong enough, or supple enough, to cope with the level of work required. If taking his work to a new pitch makes him tense, presume the harder work is the reason for the tension. Resume the easier work, and concentrate on exercises that will make him strong enough for the next level. You need to make sure he is always fully ready for the next level of work before you ask for it. Never teach something new or difficult when the horse is tired.

Bad behaviour

Sometimes a horse may behave badly and you know that the reason is tension. Something may have frightened him, or he may be tense for another reason. You may feel that it really isn't worth working your horse when he is like this. Perhaps you have been there before, and it didn't matter how long you worked him, he wouldn't behave. Scolding him certainly never made him behave better.

On occasions like this the very worst thing you could do is stop working him. This effectively rewards him for wrong behaviour. It is essential that you carry on work until he is well behaved again, even if only for a short while. You must always finish on a good note because that is where you will start the next time. Stretch your imagination to find ways of making him behave. Ask him for very easy work. Change the place that you work if there is somewhere else that he feels more secure. Stroke him and talk to him to calm him down. Try singing to him – this may calm him, or maybe not! Perhaps if you worked him in walk on a long rein for a while he might be better. There are so many reasons why a horse could be badly behaved, and so many potential cures, it is impossible to mention them all here. You must get to know your horse and learn what should help him.

Only when he has given you some good work should you finish the lesson. It doesn't matter what tactics you use to produce the good work, as long as you get it. As long as you win.

Riding a horse unsympathetically or even cruelly, shouting at him or beating him repeatedly: all of these cause the horse to worry about whether they are going to happen again, and the consequence is tension.

Horses can appear to be two personalities at once. They can be both tense, and at the same time disobedient or naughty. The one seems to grow out of the other. Like many humans, because they are frightened or tense they become confused and sometimes aggressive. When the horse becomes badly behaved, it is easy to overlook the fact that fear made him like this in the first place, and to scold him for his naughtiness. Unfortunately this increases his fear and makes the behaviour worse. This is why it is so important to try and keep the horse happy, not by giving in to him, but by understanding him. You must ask him to do what you want in a way that he will understand and find easy – mentally and physically.

It is important to recognise the horse who is naughty because of fear, as distinct from the horse who is naughty just because he is naughty. If the fearful horse misbehaves, keep cool. Calm him down. Then, quietly and firmly, explain to him again what you want him to do and ask him to do it again. If what you have asked may be a little hard for him, ask him to do something similar, but easier.

If your horse or his behaviour frightens you, or makes you tense or angry, it shows in the way you handle him. You *must* overcome these emotions before you continue working, because they make you rough or unsure in your actions and your horse will react badly. If you are rough, it will frighten him or make him tense. This will make him behave badly. If you are nervous, he knows it. He can tell that you are not a confident, strong person able to look after him and tell him what to do. This confuses him, makes him feel insecure, and his behaviour becomes even worse. Always ride calmly and confidently. You pass these feelings onto your horse and make him calm and confident too. If you are frightened or angry, and reveal these emotions, you make him fearful. You must be a good actor and become a calm, confident person. The Method school of acting is preferred. You should try and turn yourself into a calm person, rather than *pretending* to be one.

Tense riders

If a rider is tense the horse knows. The rider's legs grip the horse's sides and so he feels the tension of the rider through the legs as they grip. He thinks the rider wants him to go forwards more. So off he goes. This probably makes the rider feel even more nervous and grab the reins, which in turn will make the horse even more tense. Also, a tense rider does not flex his back. As he comes down onto the saddle he doesn't absorb his own body weight properly. He comes down heavily on the horse's spine. This also upsets the horse, possibly hurts him and, quite understandably, makes him tense.

A horse ridden like this cannot be happy. He is uncomfortable because of the gripping, the tight reins and/or the rigid back of the rider. The tension of the rider comes through to the horse immediately, because horses are so well attuned to the feel of our bodies. The horse wonders what there is to be tense about, and he too becomes tense. Unless the rider can relax, and ride in a relaxed manner, the horse cannot be relaxed. Hence a tense rider causes a horse to become tense. If a horse is ridden by a tense rider for a long time, he may become permanently tense. He may take on the personality of his trainer.

A tense rider does not make decisions well and is afraid of the horse. This fear may show in aggression or impatience. Try and recognise fear in yourself, and avoid the temptation to react against the horse. It could well be that you are both frightened of each other! It is not unusual to see a nervous person hit out at a horse that has frightened them. Quite often the cause of the incident is a tense horse, reacting nervously by shying, or lifting his head, or stepping sideways, or some other misdemeanour. This frightens the nervous rider or handler who hits the horse in retaliation, feeling the horse has been naughty. Inevitably this leads the horse to be even more nervous and tense. If the rider only had the sense to realise that the horse was tense in the first place, he would stroke and soothe the horse rather than making the tension worse by hitting him. You can probably recognise occasions when you have been a little unsure of, or intimidated by, a horse. You became tense and unable to ride and treat the horse as well as you ought. If a horse makes you nervous, it is indeed difficult to remain calm and handle him confidently. But, if you are anything less than calm, you will make him even more frightened and even more frightening. It is back to acting, and pretending to be calm even when you are not.

Wind

Horses, particularly those with a tendency to nervousness, frequently become tense when it is windy. Their hearing is impaired by the noise of the wind. Sounds, which would normally be audible to them, are carried away on the wind, or drowned out by the noise of the wind. A horse's hearing is normally very acute. He uses this facility in the wild, and in domesticated life, to keep him safe. If a potential threat were obscured from sight the horse would hear it. Knowing he is so well able to hear makes him more relaxed. Deprived of his ability to hear by the wind, he becomes over-alert, reacting to everything that moves. He tries to substitute sight for hearing, and will twitch this way and that to see all around him. Naturally, he is nervous and tense because he has less warning of a predator's approach. He is constantly on the alert and ready to flee. This tension is a self-protection mechanism.

Frequent exposure (see page 219) is unlikely to work with wind. To be nervous when he cannot hear is so much a part of a horse's nature that no amount of exposure to wind will convince him that he is safe.

A horse who is well disciplined and trusts his rider is better behaved in the wind than other horses. Even so, his level of concentration is often affected by the attention he diverts in trying to hear over the noise of the wind, and see what he cannot hear.

Incorrect or over-feeding (particularly rich grass in spring)

If the horse's digestive system is overloaded with rich spring grass (or sometimes early autumn grass), or too much hard feed, it produces toxins that will make him crazy. The differing metabolism of horses makes this problem less in some horses than in others. Fine bodied, thoroughbred types tend to suffer less than heavier built horses whose metabolism is slower.

If your horse is affected by rich grass, reduce its availability or put him on poorer pasture. Or consider using a magnesium supplement (see page 273).

It is easy to overdo the amount of hard feed. This will also cause horses to be excitable. Our natural desire to do the best for our horses often leads us to over feed them, rather like an indulgent mother feeding her increasingly obese children. If your horse has been made crazy by too much feed, reduce it to an absolute minimum, perhaps only feeding hay. Keep it there for several days. If too much feed is causing the problem, you should begin to notice a difference and sanity should start returning. If, on this lower level of feed, the horse maintains his physical condition, and has enough energy for the work he is doing, keep to it. However, if he loses condition, or doesn't have sufficient energy, increase the hard feed by a small amount. Every two or three days, gradually step up the feed level, until you reach the point where it supplies him with sufficient energy for the work you wish him to do, but without returning to silly behaviour. The diet you choose must suit your horse as an individual. There is no guide that can be given as to amounts of feed, because each horse's requirements are so different.

Strange surroundings or circumstances
A horse who has never been to a competition or any gathering of horses before will naturally be nervous of all the activity, and the presence of so many horses doing strange things. This tends to pass after the horse has been to several such occasions in close succession (frequent exposure). Some horses panic when seeing sheep, or donkeys (particularly braying ones), at close quarters for the first time. Most horses are thrown into a complete fit when they see pigs. If they see them frequently, they may become less upset by them, although the fear of pigs is often maintained even then.

Rider's lack of discipline

Either the rider or the horse must be the dominant partner in the relationship. If the rider does not assert his dominance, then it follows that the horse is the dominant one. In this case, the horse only does as the rider wants when it suits him. He believes that he is in control of the situation (as he is) and therefore is responsible for what happens. Because of this, he, instead of the rider, has to make the decisions. This often causes the horse to be nervous and insecure.

This is a little bit like an adult and a child going into a potentially dangerous situation together. For example, crossing the road. If the adult is in charge, the child feels relaxed, relying on the competence and knowledge of the older person. Normally the adult holds the child's hand securely, and totally takes over. The child relaxes because he trusts the adult, who, carefully and calmly, takes them both safely across the road. If the child were crossing the road on his own, he would be agitated and tense, looking from side to side and studying the road. When he judged it safe, he would probably run across to the other side. He would not enjoy the experience. His heart may be pounding afterwards. In the same way, if the horse felt dominated by the rider, he would relax. This is because he knows the rider is strong, will make the right decisions, and will look after him. He does not worry about what to do next. The rider will tell him. If he thinks the rider won't tell him, if he has to make all the decisions himself, he will be tense.

Discipline

Sometimes horses misbehave and you have to discipline them, either by smacking or by raising your voice. Some horses, particularly those of a sensitive nature, get upset if they are disciplined, even if they deserve it. Some of them then behave worse than before! You may often presume that this bad behaviour is further naughtiness, so naturally you scold him again. This makes his behaviour worse still. But, in fact this second misdemeanour is caused by tension, because he is upset at being scolded. After the first discipline, which perhaps cannot be avoided, immediately make up with your horse. Remind him that you still love him with a stroke and a gentle word. If he is this sensitive type of horse, he requires very little in the way of discipline. A verbal reprimand will often be sufficient.

Rider's inconsistency
The rider needs to make it absolutely clear what he wants. If he is unclear in the aids, or incapable of insisting that the horse is obedient to the aids, this can result in a confused horse. He does not know what the rider wants, and therefore has to make some of the decisions himself. It is much easier for a horse if the rider is in control. The horse can then relax. A consistent rider tends to produce a calmer horse. Your horse must always know what you want him to do and that you will insist on his doing it.

Unnatural lifestyle
A horse cooped up for days, weeks, months or even years on end in a stable, only being allowed out for work, is much more likely to suffer from tension than a horse allowed to graze most days.

Anticipation
A horse may become tense because he is expecting something to happen which he very much likes, or very much dislikes. For example, suppose you are teaching your horse a new manoeuvre, one with which he has physical or mental difficulty. Asking him to perform it may make him tense – this is understandable. But, he may also be tense because he *thinks* you are going to ask him to perform it, even if you haven't mentioned it to him. Perhaps you have worked on it every day at about the same time and it is approaching that time now. He may be expecting it and this expectation makes him tense. Perhaps you have already asked him for it, and are now moving onto something different, but he is still expecting it.

Anticipating something good can also make a horse tense. The other day I rode my horse at a different time from usual. It was in the late afternoon, before she had had her feed. My normally quiet animal was doing everything at such a rate of knots. She thought her feed would be in the stable when she returned, and she couldn't wait to get to it. Strangely, I experienced a similar sensation shortly afterwards when I was preparing my own food. I was hungry and it looked so tempting, I found myself rushing the preparation. The anticipation of the food had definitely made me tense. Horses are nearly always tense just before feed arrives, or before they go outside. A gelding I have always stales just before he has his feed and just before he goes outside – a strange way of showing tension but not uncommon! Some horses are tense just before you ride them, and misbehave when you are tacking them up. Whether this is because they are anticipating a good experience or a bad one I am not sure!

Cures for tension
Tension increases the speed at which the heart beats. We can try to lower the heart rate and relax the horse by stroking him on his withers, just as an equine grooming friend might do. This is particularly useful when you are riding, as your hands are right by his withers. Talking to him in a soothing voice can also induce relaxation. Sometimes the horse can be too tense to take any notice of what you are doing, Don't give up too soon, because it can sometimes take a while to cut into the tension and get through to him.

If your horse is a tense type, try to find situations in which he is less tense. Use these for training, perhaps after he has been out at grass for an hour or two. A horse who has been out grazing will often be more relaxed than a horse who has been stabled for hours or days. If there is much grass on the field, beware of damaging the lungs. The stomach lies near to the lungs. When the horse works, his lungs need to expand to provide more oxygen for his working body. If the stomach is full, there is less room for the lungs to expand, putting strain on the existing lung capacity and possibly causing damage.

If you need to take advantage of a full stomach to gain a quiet horse, keep the work undemanding, and never let the horse's breathing become at all fast. The most practical way is to ride your horse perhaps half an hour after he has been fed a smallish feed of concentrates, when the stomach is no longer full, but the horse doesn't yet feel hungry again. Think of the rather contented feeling you have after a meal. You are much less likely to be edgy and tense then. But, because your stomach is full, you don't feel too much like running round either. Half an hour later would be better.

If your horse spends too much time in the stable with nothing to do, put him out in a field more often or for longer. If he lacks company, particularly equine, give him some. If his way of life is close to nature he has more chance of having a relaxed personality.

The thinking rider
It is up to you as a thinking rider to work out why your horse is tense and, if possible, try to devise methods of making him less tense.

Tiring the horse
One would imagine that a tired horse would be less tense, but, for some unfathomable reason, horses always seem to have enough energy to be tense; in fact, being tired quite often makes them more tense.

Use of tranquillisers
These do have the desired effect of making the horse less tense, but, unfortunately, make the horse drowsy and unable to perform safely.

Magnesium depletion
When the horse is suffering from magnesium depletion he can become very tense. A horse suffering from hypomagnesemia can also be irritable, unwilling and generally not his usual self. This tension can last for a long time – until he has sufficient magnesium in his system again. Stress can cause the horse to lose more magnesium from his system than normal. Circumstances such as a change of routine, cold weather, an accident, his first few competitions, travelling (particularly on a long journey), very hard work or

any kind of a stressful or frightening situation can cause such a loss. Unfortunately, modern farming methods tend not to provide sufficient levels of magnesium to allow this depletion to be restored naturally.

Magnesium deficiency can also be caused by rich grass, or over-feeding of concentrates.

There are several products on the market containing magnesium. They can have a magic effect on the temperament of a horse suffering a deficiency. Within a matter of days he should be back to his normal self. I personally have used a product by Triple Crown called NOMAD that contains partly chelated, and therefore easily absorbed, magnesium. For information on availability see the Appendix (page 283). If you have a horse who gets tense in certain situations, such as a show, consider feeding him a supplement of magnesium for a few days beforehand.

Herbal, homeopathic and probiotic remedies
Some people swear by them – others find them useless. The answer must be to try them and see how they suit your horse.

There is another product manufactured by Triple Crown which deals with tension in horses, called Attitude Adjuster. Not having any knowledge or experience of the product, I was keen to test it, particularly before I was prepared to recommend it here! I tried it on a horse of my own and persuaded two other people to try it on their tense animals. In all three horses the results were very impressive. After 10 days to a fortnight they were all saner and more relaxed.

One of the horses was problematic all the time, but particularly when being ridden: not staying still when being mounted and spooking at everything on the road. This particular horse also box-walked constantly, leaving his stable in a dreadful mess. After about a fortnight on Attitude Adjuster he improved in every way. Even though he was by no means perfect, there was a marked difference and he became much easier to handle and ride. It may be that his bad behaviour had become so much a way of life for him that, to some degree, he was still behaving like this out of habit, even though the reason for the behaviour, the tension, had gone.

The second horse, a mare, is one who takes her work very seriously and allows it to make her tense. After ten days on Attitude Adjuster she was coping with her work in a much more relaxed manner.

The third horse (my own) was a gelding who I was in the process of backing. When I was lungeing him he would sometimes be naughty. I would scold him, and everything went wrong from that point. He couldn't cope with discipline, yet sometimes he just had to have it. There seemed no way forward until I tried Attitude Adjuster. When he was on it he was much calmer and his behaviour improved dramatically. He was rarely naughty and, if he did misbehave, he then coped well with being disciplined. Three out of three seems a pretty good average. I think I could recommend you give it a try.

I have not heard of or experienced any side-effects of any of the contents of Attitude Adjuster but cannot vouch for their absence.

I am told by the manufacturers that it is of no use on mares who suffer from cyclical tension, but it is very good on horses who manifest their tension by becoming withdrawn and becoming quiet and slower in performance. I was also told by the manufacturers that, if it was necessary to feed the product long term, it may be possible to reduce the dosage gradually. They suggested sticking with each reduced dosage for approximately a week before cutting it down further. If the symptoms returned during that week, return the dosage to the higher one.

16

What Do Horses Enjoy?

Or, more accurately, do horses enjoy anything? And, if so, why?

Because we love horses, we like to do things to make them happy: a nice big feed, a warm stable and/or rug, the company of other horses, turning out on a sunny spring day onto a field full of fresh grass. This list is based on what a horse needs for survival: warmth, food and the protection of a group. We enjoy things which we need to survive, so we presume that it is the same for horses. We like the idea that our friends enjoy themselves.

What if we tried adding to this list other things that we enjoy, and feel our horse also enjoys? Galloping with other horses, jumping, hacking out. Are we now in the realms of fantasy? *We* enjoy them so we refer our enjoyment to the horse. Are we right to make this presumption? They have no need to do these things to survive (except in certain circumstances) but some horses do appear to enjoy themselves at these times. Is it possible to gain some insight into the minds of horses who appear to enjoy some things more than others? Jumping, for example: some horses seem to love it while others exhibit no inclination to jump unless forced.

Why is there this difference? Is it purely liking and disliking, as some people like apples and others don't, or are there more practical reasons? Do some horses dislike jumping because they are less athletic and therefore have a physical disadvantage? Or is it because they have been trained roughly or badly so that they have a fear of it? Both of these would be understandable reasons. But do some horses dislike or like things for no particular reason?

Some horses appear to enjoy racing. They strive to get to the front of the field. There are others who hang back. They are difficult to persuade to make even the slightest effort to get in front of another horse. You might think that perhaps these animals are naturally slow, but this is not the case. Those same horses who want to be behind are not necessarily slow movers when they are on their own. They just don't like being in front of others. Physical reasons do not explain this. If they can go fast when on their own, then in company they have no physical reason to go slow. We, therefore, have to presume that it is the mentality of the horse that inhibits his performance. He simply doesn't like it. Just as some people like golf and others don't.

What about the flat race trainer, who has had horse after horse through his hands and started them all racing? He treated and trained every horse in exactly the same way. They were all bred to race and should have the physical ability. How else could you explain the reason behind their often very differing performances, if not that they either liked or disliked the sport?

We humans need to be constantly on our guard against anthropomorphism with animals. Inevitably, when someone says horses are behaving like humans, the scientific mind immediately wants to reject it. But perhaps, sometimes, we are correct to assume they behave like humans. After all, humans have been able to subdue and ride horses for thousands of years. One reason is the similarities of our two species.

We know that circumstances can cause a horse to dislike certain things. If so, logic suggests it is possible to make a horse like something which he otherwise would not like. For example, if, every time your horse jumps a jump, he is given a pat or a carrot, he learns to associate jumping with nice things. Eventually he may well think he likes jumping, even if he didn't before. This tactic has wider relevance.

Conditioning by pleasure really comes into its own during schooling. If everything that happens during and around the hard or boring work is really pleasant – rests, praise and perhaps treats – the horse thinks of training sessions as pleasurable. The whole atmosphere of training changes. It should become an uplifting experience for both horse and rider. If you weren't already, you should now be working together as a partnership.

Does the horse have any sense of his owner's enjoyment? If the rider is enthusiastic about, shall we say, hacking out, perhaps the horse picks up some of his owner's happiness and shares it. This is probably an overstatement. More likely the horse enjoys the natural consequences of his rider's joy, such as a pat or an extra feed, and associates that with the hacking out. Even more likely, the horse really does enjoy hacking out, because there is nothing much demanded physically or mentally.

Do horses love?
Again we are back to anthropomorphism. We love them so we want them to behave like us and love us back. We would like to think of them as loyal, thinking creatures who, like Champion the Wonder Horse, would come and save us in threatening situations. Although this is definitely stretching reality, there are some horses who do make enormous efforts for their riders, well above and beyond the call of duty.

Horses certainly do display some kind of feeling for humans. Even when there is no feed bowl about, they often watch their owner if they are separated, and nicker happily when they are re-united. There are even some horses who go into decline if separated from their owners for long. So perhaps there is emotion. But would it be fanciful to say that this emotion is love?

First we need to define love. The most obvious kind is based on sexual attraction, which we can discount here. There is also the non-sexual love one could have for a friend. This could be based on shared interests and respect. Then there is the love one has for one's children, which is based on maternal/paternal love and the survival of the species. We are programmed to love our children like this so that we will protect our young. In parallel, there is also the love a child has for its parent. This love is engendered by the need for security and for caring, strong company. Children are programmed to love the provider of food, warmth, shelter and protection. Such love makes sense if you wish to survive. Now we are getting nearer to the relationship which horses have for other horses. It is based on survival. Finding food, the need of company for protection. If we have supplanted the role of other horses in the life of our horse then it does not take too great a leap of faith to believe that we have come to occupy the emotional relationship that they have for one another. How close it is to the human emotion termed love, we shall never know.

We have seen how horses are givers and receivers of affection when they bond with each other. They display a strong need to belong, and to feel they are cared for. Children give ponies masses of attention and affection. When we grow older, we often presume that, because they are animals, they don't really need this affection. As children we gave it only to satisfy our own desire to give love. But perhaps we are wrong. Perhaps they do like this affection and respond by giving affection in return. If you watch children with their ponies, they certainly do seem to enjoy a very special and rewarding relationship.

During my research for this book I have deliberately increased the amount of care and affection I give to my horses. I have certainly noticed a difference in their attitudes towards me. I enjoy their company more and they are happier because of our changed relationship. As well as being caring to them when I handle them, I am more sympathetic when they are being schooled. I seldom get cross with them. I always take more time to explain things carefully. I don't push them as hard as I used to. I rest them more often if work is stressful. I praise more, and stop work if I feel they have had enough. It all boils down to loving them more and caring about them as individuals. I would never have believed that it could make so much difference to their behaviour and their well-being.

The title of this chapter is "What do horses enjoy?". One thing is for certain. They enjoy being loved and treated kindly, and repay doubly the care that they are given.

17

The Nature of the Rider

The expert rider is armed with many skills and much knowledge. A teacher, able to communicate with his horse and understand his communications, and an athlete with the skill and physical ability to ride and school a horse correctly. You are working to produce an animal who has the strength of a body builder with the beauty and grace of a ballet dancer. To create this altered and enhanced animal, you need to understand the mechanics of his motion and balance. You must combine the emotions and skills of a carer and teacher – befriending and loving your horse – with the strengths of a strict master.

Understanding your own nature is important in your ability to train a horse. People are all different, and therefore the relationship you have with your horse differs from the relationship another person would have. It is important to understand your personality and how you relate to your horse. You need to evaluate your strengths and weaknesses so as to build upon the former and improve the latter.

It is worth studying the natures and temperaments of successful riders to see if they have anything in common. Is there a temperament that is most suited to the training of horses? Do successful riders have characteristics that we can try and emulate?

Calmness and patience would probably come highest in the list of desirable characteristics and are the most commonly noticed virtues. Being calm, and thinking rather than over-reacting, helps the horse stay calm. It also helps the rider to make the sanest decision if things start to go wrong.

The successful rider has the ability, natural or acquired, to dominate his horse. He instils in the horse the knowledge that the rider is boss and the horse must always do as he is told. He is not cruel nor needs he violence to obtain obedience or establish domination.

Determination and tenacity are also high on the list. Schooling a horse takes time and there are often setbacks. You must weather the many storms. You cannot give up when things go wrong. A determined rider will try and try again.

A most undesirable characteristic would be impatience or any tendency to short temper. Losing your temper with an animal is always counterproductive.

The ability to bond with the horse and to empathise with his thoughts and feelings is common to most successful trainers. They love and care for their horses almost like their own children. They make sure that everything is right with them. A happy and contented horse who trusts his trainer will give so much more than an unhappy or distrustful horse.

There can't be a successful trainer who isn't also brave. You risk being thrown off when scolding a naughty horse. You are fearless and always assertive in the presence of a potential bullying monster.

You may not have all these characteristics naturally. But, with determination, you can acquire them. Through self-discipline you can become more patient, and with motivation a lot of the rest can be learnt.

Tension in riders is a bar to relaxed, sensitive riding. It could be caused by nerves or, perversely, by too much motivation. Over-motivated riders will over ride their horse – push, push, pushing all the time. It wears them out, it wears their horses out and, because there is so much tension, it doesn't even work well. The rider must make a conscious effort to relax. It can help to sing or hum in the rhythm of the horse's gait. The advantages to being a relaxed rider are that the seat is deeper and the reactions calmer. The horse should be calmer, too, and the rider should have a better feel of how the horse is going.

A great asset so far unmentioned is talent, the intuitive gift of understanding what to do when and how to do it. It is arbitrarily allocated in different quantities to different people! If you don't possess it, the only alternative is hard work, based on the advice given in books like this.

Appendix

Triple Crown products are currently available at some feed and tack shops and through:

Stable Express mail order
26 Pillings Road
Oakham
Rutland
LE15 6QF
Freephone 0800 7831404

The Society of Teachers of the Alexander Technique
1st Floor
Linton House
39–51 Highgate Road
London
NW5 1RS
0845 230 7828
www.stat.org.uk

Index